Brindley Hosken is a farmer who has lived and farmed by the beautiful Helford riveron the Lizard peninsula in Cornwall for all of his life. He has been married to Ruth for thirty-seven years and they have three children and five grand-children. Brindley has served as a parish Councillor for thirty-five years. He was a school Governor for eight years and is currently Vice President of Cornwall Young Farmers Club. His first book, Cows and Catastrophes, was published six years ago.

This book is dedicated to my present and future grandchildren. I hope in the future it will give them a connection from the future to the past.

To

Jasper Hosken

Ross Carter

Harvey Hosken

Dana Carter

Gracie Hosken.

Brindley Hosken

UP LONG MEADOW

AUSTIN MACAULEY PUBLISHERS™
LONDON • CAMBRIDGE • NEW YORK • SHARJAH

Copyright © Brindley Hosken 2023

The right of Brindley Hosken to be identified as author of this work has been asserted by the author in accordance with sections 77 and 78 of the Copyright, Designs and Patents Act 1988.

All rights reserved. No part of this publication may be reproduced, stored in a retrieval system, or transmitted in any form or by any means, electronic, mechanical, photocopying, recording, or otherwise, without the prior permission of the publishers.

Any person who commits any unauthorised act in relation to this publication may be liable to criminal prosecution and civil claims for damages.

This is a work of fiction. Names, characters, businesses, places, events, locales, and incidents are either the products of the author's imagination or used in a fictitious manner. Any resemblance to actual persons, living or dead, or actual events is purely coincidental.

A CIP catalogue record for this title is available from the British Library.

ISBN 9781035806713 (Paperback)
ISBN 9781035806720 (Hardback)
ISBN 9781035806737 (ePub e-book)

www.austinmacauley.com

First Published 2023
Austin Macauley Publishers Ltd®
1 Canada Square
Canary Wharf
London
E14 5AA

Up Long Meadow

Five years ago, my first book, 'Cows and Catastrophes', was published. I was very pleased that I could even write a book and even more pleased that I could get it published. In the last three years, I have somehow reached the age of sixty and managed to acquire three grandsons and in the last twelve months a granddaughter. The three boys are from five years down and already showing their different personalities. Jasper, slightly anxious and awkward. I look at him and see shades of myself. Ross, who talks about the crescent moon and has a wide streak of cussedness in him.

Harvey, who has to test every boundary that he is given, just to see if you mean it. Little Dana Grace who walks towards me to sit on my knee, stops just out of reach, shakes her head and walks away with a cheeky smile. With two of them living on the farm and the other two living eight miles away, we have the joy of watching them develop. I look at them and wonder what life will hold for them. Will they continue as the next generation of many generations of farmers, or will they be seduced by a regular job, five- day week, every weekend off and a company pension?

It may already be too late, as they farm the sand pit with their many tractors and get their granny to be 'Digger Man', and load up all their trailers with sand, to be transported across the yard to another imaginary farm. Of all the pedal tractors we have accumulated, the thirty years old Massey that we gave their father for Christmas seems to be the favourite. No pedals and various holes and dents in it, but they seem to know instinctively where to drive to get the most speed as they race down the yard. Usually getting to the bottom, but sometimes coming to grief on the way.

I remember my grandfather saying, if we had hurt ourselves, "Shall I spit on that to make it better?" I find myself asking the same question, "Shall I spit on that to make it better?"

What will farming in this little piece of Cornwall look like, by the time they leave school and start to make their way in life? Will I still be here to see it? Will the vociferous minority have got their way, banned livestock farming and saved the planet with their inflammatory language and sterile lives? Will the hills that my father and Uncle cleared to make more grassland be once more planted in trees, to soak up carbon?

Either way, we that farm the land, will continue to do so, dealing with the problems and opportunities as they arise. Doing what makes economic sense at the time and understanding that nothing is permanent in farming.

This book is for my grandchildren and I hope in the years to come, they will read and appreciate the story it tells. The stories written are how I remember them being told to me, memories becoming subjective over time. They will show how farming has changed during the course of my working life at Withan Farm. I have tried to take myself back to the various stages of my life. Times of rampant testosterone, times of extreme anxiety, times of debilitating stress and depression, times of complete joy. The highs and lows from nearly fifty years of farming in this bit of Cornwall that I have loved and always called home.

St Martin in Meneage

St Martin in Meneage is a small parish bordering the South side of the Helford River, some six miles from Helston. A good agricultural parish with fertile soils capable of growing pretty much anything, and I would guess, enjoying the mildest climate of anywhere in the country. I have been a parish councillor in St Martin for thirty-five years and was a school governor for eight years. I feel like the boy with his finger in the dyke trying to slow down the pace of change, but failing miserably, as the powers that be decide what will happen to the Community assets in our village.

I suppose the catalyst for change in our village, as well as many others in the area are second homes. I can understand it.

Character Cottage in St Martin, a mile from the magnificent sailing waters of the Helford River and in an area of outstanding natural beauty. A snip at £400,000!

St Martin avoided this phenomenon for many years, unlike the neighbouring villages of Manaccan and more especially Helford, where during the winter the village has been practically empty for many years.

Unfortunately, second homes bring nothing to the parish. They remain empty for nine months and are usually only occupied in the summer, Christmas and Easter. There are no children from these houses skipping to the school, no women popping to the shop for odds and ends and a catch up (sexist comment Brin). No help to foster community spirit. I drive through the village in winter. The lived- in houses are bright with light, but the second homes appear dark and dead, an irritation to me, but I have no answers.

One of our community assets were three local-needs homes built for senior citizens. These were built about thirty-five years ago, just as I became a parish councillor. I was very proud of them. Two one- bedroom flats and one two- bedroom flat, all on one level. Ideal for local residents who due to changed circumstances in their life just needed a small flat in the small community where they had lived all their lives. For thirty years that is actually what they were used for and it did my heart good as I knew who lived in each one, for all of those thirty years.

Five years ago, the two- bedroom flat became empty. As a parish council, we passed on to the Housing Association, who owned them, names of local people who had expressed an interest in living there. Nothing happened for a couple of years, the flat being left empty. We then heard rumours that it was going to be sold. Not possible, I thought, there were covenants on them restricting them to local needs. The rumours proved to be true and although I went to two County Council planning meetings to argue against the restrictions being lifted, in the end the housing association got their way, arguing that the house was in a poor state of repair and would result in fuel poverty. Thirty years old and in a poor state of repair. I despaired. Two of the flats have now been sold and the third will eventually go down the same route I have no doubt. One more nail in the coffin of local life.

The primary school at St Martin was the beating hub of the village. I was edukated there, as were my three children, my aunt, various cousins and nephews and nieces. Many of the friends I made at primary school are still my friends today. Before my time, local children who did not go to grammar school would stay at St Martin school until the age of fourteen, when they would leave school to begin work on the local farms or for local trades men. During my time at St Martin, local parents raised money and built a swimming pool at the school.

Most local children learned to swim in that pool and parents would take turns in opening it during the summer holidays to allow the local children to have a swim. By the time my children started school, health and safety regulations were being brought in. We erected a solid wood fence around the pool in order to keep it open, but in a couple of years that was not deemed sufficient and the pool had to be knocked down and filled in. It did not feel like progress.

As many local rural schools know, numbers of pupils are cyclical and alter from year to year. In my year, there were three of us. In my son's year, some thirty years later, there were twelve of them. Whenever school numbers were low, school closure was suggested, but as a parish, parents and school governors, we always managed to avoid this happening, as have many other schools on the Lizard Peninsula.

Unfortunately, in the last cyclical low, things had changed. The school was run by an academy. The governors were now "partners in learning". Economically, closure looked a good idea to the academy, with no local connections. As a local community, we did our best to point out the cyclical nature of small schools and spent a lot of time at the school tidying things up in the grounds, which had been allowed to slip. We also pointed out the number of younger children in the pipeline, my grandchildren among them. To no avail. The school closed two years ago and has now been made into a house. It will probably be called The Old Schoolhouse. My grandsons ride past it every day on their way to pre-school in the neighbouring village of Garras.

In the centre of the village, the blacksmiths and carpenters shop have gone, to be replaced by a small village green and houses. The villagers themselves come and go over the years and whereas I used to know the majority of parishioners, I now know very few, with houses changing hands with monotonous regularity.

Although the village has changed considerably in my time, the farms have changed little. Small farms have been taken over. Systems have changed, some intensifying, some extensifying. Some still milking cows, some no longer milking cows. Some diversifying, some concentrating on their core business. Many letting part of the farmhouse to self-catering visitors. BUT

>The Blee's still farm Trenower.
>The Bray's still farm Tregevis.
>The Bryant's still farm Sworne.
>The Hosken's still farm Withan.
>The Hosking's still farm Gear.
>The Jenkin's still farm Mudgeon.
>The William's still farm Tretharrup.

The same families farming the same land, for at least the last seventy years.

What the parish will look like in another sixty years, is anybody's guess.

Will the same families be farming in St Martin?

Will there be any local residents (three generations in the graveyard) left?

Will all the local rural schools be still open or will they be replaced with one large school covering the whole of the Lizard Peninsula?

What changes will my grandchildren see in St Martin in their lives?

Helston Cattle Market

Helston Cattle Market is situated at the bottom of the town and served local farmers for hundreds of years. In my time it was run by three local auctioneering firms.

    Jose Collins and Harris
    Michell and Nicholls
    John Coad and Son.

These three firms used to sell calves, store cattle and fat cattle through three rings, alternating which group of cattle they sold each week. There was also a shed for pigs, but by the time I left school, there were rarely any pigs sold. In the 1950s and '60s most farms had several pigs, our farm among them. By the 1970s, pig production was more and more concentrated on specialist pig farms and it was no longer deemed economic to have just a half dozen sows, as farms started to specialise.

Around the edge of the market grounds, were a series of wooden huts. These were run by local Agricultural firms, such as Cornwall Farmers, NFU, Cornish Mutual Colin Delbridge and Michael Boaden. These enabled farmers, while at market, to conduct some business, pay a bill or get a quote for fertiliser, machinery or seeds.

Opposite the market was a set of steps leading up to the town. At the top of the steps was Coinage Hall, where our local veterinary practise, Head and Head, was based. Very handy if you needed some cattle medicine to take home. A little farther up Coinage Hall Street was the bank, once again handy if you needed to pay a cheque in. Our usual practise was to then go to the chip shop for dinner and then home to do some work.

The steps leading up from the market must have had many generations of farmers traversing them over the decades. (I have seen a photo of my great-grandfather standing at the top of these steps with his market clothes on. Waistcoat, jacket, pocket watch and gaiters.)

To the right of the market is a track called Bullock Lane. This was used to drive the cattle to market before the advent of cattle lorries and avoided all the cattle travelling through the town. This track is still in existence and I have walked it recently. Part of it has been built on and a couple of new roads to bisect it. I wonder if anyone who walks on it now has given any thought to why it is so named?

Even farther back in the mists of time, there was a gang of highway men and footpads called the Windmill Gang. In the 1820s they would waylay farmers coming home from the market and rob and beat them. This was around Drytree on Goonhilly Downs. Nowadays, you can drive through Goonhilly Downs in about three minutes, along the wide straight road, past the mighty satellite dishes put up in the fifties and on to St Keverne.

It does not take much imagination, however, to go back two hundred years, a late foggy afternoon in November, a narrow single track unmade road, no lights from the satellite station. Just a three mile stretch of dark unpopulated downsland, with the risk of being set on by the ungodly. They must have breathed a sigh of relief after passing through. The Windmill gang were eventually caught, and two of them were hanged for their transgressions.

I remember as a young boy having a gaberdine mac passed down to me. It was too big for me and I could not wait until I was big enough to wear it to market. I would look like a proper farmer! (Nowadays, I wonder how not to look like a farmer!) I cannot remember if I ever got to wear that mac to market, the thrill was in the waiting, the anticipation.

Just after I left school, we sent five Hereford store cattle to market. Stores were well grown cattle that were sold to another farmer for fattening. On that day they sold really well. £206 a piece. So well, that as I walked up to the town, farmers were saying, "you did all right today, boy. What are you going to do with all that money?"

Ironically, the man who bought those stores, Mr Dennis Bray of Constantine, later had a grandson, who thirty years later married my daughter!

Many farmers would attend Helston Market every Monday, while their wives were up in the town doing the weekly shopping. If the market was doing well, the town was doing well. Helston market drew farmers from all over the Lizard Peninsula, as well as some from Falmouth and Penzance.

Helston Market closed in 2005, as did many of the smaller markets at Penzance, Camborne and Redruth. I suppose the death knell was the BSE (mad cow disease) crisis. This brought in a lot more restrictions that the smaller markets struggled to cope with. Helston Market had a good atmosphere and the majority of farmers who attended would be known or at least acquainted to you. It is only when such places are gone out of your life that you realise their importance. The camaraderie, social interaction and banter that is missing from your farming life and the few chances you now have to mix with your contemporaries.

There is practically one livestock market left in Cornwall at Truro. Moved from the City and built on a greenfield site almost forty years ago, it is undoubtedly more efficient, large salerings, high roof and plenty of room for everyone. But cold! Cold physically and cold mentally. At least to me! I have been there and not seen anyone I know, which is why I have not been there for the last ten years.

Helston Market is now a skate park and there is a small community centre there. It is called The Old Cattle Market

Isn't that nice!

Harvest.

One of my children once asked me if I could remember the Great Fire of London! I could not and I could not remember binders cutting the corn, but I do remember a combine being pulled by a tractor with approximately a five feet cutter bar. The disadvantage of this set up, was the necessity to drive on the crop while opening up the field. This would have been during the mid-sixties. This combine was superseded by a self-propelled combine that had a seven-foot header and a slide at the back to slide the hundredweight (50 Kilo) bags of grain onto the field in piles, where they would be picked up and transported to the barn. The slide could also be used by children!

The next combine was a Massey Ferguson 780 Special. This combine had a tool box just behind the driver's seat. This tool box would hold two small children, who would sit there watching proceedings, as the drum belt spun furiously a foot to their right. This was the first combine I ever drove. With an eight- foot six- inch cutter bar and bulk grain instead of bags, already in the mid-seventies the hard physical work was starting to be done away with.

There was no cab on the 780. The black dust and shimmering heat would swirl up from the cutter bar with every breath of wind and encase your neck and face. The barley awns would get down your shirt and itch and scratch. By the end of the day, you would be spitting black, trying to clear the dust from your lungs. Small rivulets of white would show in your face where your eyes had watered so badly trying to get rid of the dust. Terrible, terrible conditions for working.

I loved it!

What was the thrill?

It was the art of leaving the stubble as short as possible without dragging up soil. The art of leaving an even swath of straw behind with no grain left, and after the field had all been cleared of straw seeing no standing or flattened barley left in the field, making ploughing the field for the next crop a doddle. Obviously, it was not always like that and sometimes there would be weeds growing up through the crop or the crop would be flattened, either by rain or a little too much fertiliser.

These crops were a challenge to combine and I have to admit to sometimes making a mess of combining. I have not driven a combine for about twenty- five years. We did not grow a lot of corn, and combines were expensive. It made sense to have a contractor in to harvest the barley. Fifteen years ago, we stopped growing barley all together.

As with most Agricultural commodities, prices have not caught up with reality. Today barley is trading at approximately £140 per tonne and I can remember selling it for £126 per tonne more than thirty years ago. That might still be profitable on the large fields and farms in the east of the country, but on our average size field of six acres, it does not really make economic sense.

It is hard to believe that in the last fifty years, we have gone from tractor driven, five- foot cut combines, to today, where the biggest combines have up to a sixty- foot header, up to eight hundred horse power engine and have satellite navigation, which enables them to self-steer and cuts down the overlap between bouts to less than two inches. Far better than any human driver could do. Obviously, these leviathans will never be seen in my corner of Cornwall, as the narrow farm lanes and roads are the limiting factor. Ten foot is the maximum width of machinery and some roads will not take even that.

What always amazed me when combining was the part the weather played. If the sun was shining and a bit of a breeze the crop would whistle through. If a small cloud obscured the sun, you could immediately feel the difference. There would be less life in the crop and it would tangle around the front reel and the combine engine would grunt as the crop went through the drum. It was the same at the end of the day. As the sun was going down around seven thirty to eight 'o' clock, the crop would suddenly go dead.

However much you wanted to go on and finish the field, once nature said no, then no it was. Carrying on would be very frustrating as the crop would tangle around the reel and catch on the reciprocating knife and there was a real chance of causing damage to the machine.

Whether the new combines of today are robust enough to carry on and force their will on nature, I do not know, but I will always remember the WHOOOOPH, as a lump of harvested corn went over the drum of the combine and thinking, woah, that's enough for the day Brin!

Straw Harvest

In the 1970s and '80s, after I had left school, we worked with my mother's brother, Ronnie Jenkin and my father's brother, Geoffrey Hosken during silage harvest and corn harvest. The farms were Mudgeon, Withan, Treworgie, Higher Trenower, Lannarth and Trewothack. They were all within a diameter of three miles and it made sense to work together and put a good team on the job. During the corn harvesting, there would be one man driving the combine, one man tipping the grain, one man baling. The rest were left to carry the straw. The straw was all made in small bales and we would carry about 10,000 a year.

They were around four foot long and two- foot square, weighing around forty pounds. The trailers carried around one hundred and eighty bales and they were all pitched onto the trailers manually, using a two pronged pitch fork. Pitching bales was a job I really enjoyed at the time. I was fit and strong and lean. Six-foot three-inches tall and 13 stone in weight. I loved the feel of the sun on my back and the summer breeze drying the sweat as I pitched those bales, with no shirt on, getting browner every day. No real worries at that time, just the hope that tomorrow would be just as sunny.

I would have loaded bales all day, if possible, but they had to be taken into the yards and unloaded. Not so pleasant. At Trewothack, there was a stone barn on two levels. There were calves on ground level and bales were stored on the upper level, where they could be thrown down to bed the calves during the winter. The elevator that lifted the bales had an endless chain with spikes on.

This elevator would be positioned through a window in the barn and bring the bales up into the barn. As the barn was totally enclosed, there was no breeze and it would get extremely hot. As the barn filled up there was less and less space until finally there was one man left, filling the last bit of space with bales until there was no room left. Finally, gratefully coming outside for air and a cold drink.

The other difficult place at Trewothack was the silage pit. The silage had been harvested a couple of months before, had settled so was not level, especially around the sides, where it was quite spongy. Building straw bale on it was like building a house on sand. It was a matter of doing your best and trying to tie them in so they held each other in place. There was not much kudos given if the stack you were building collapsed and had to be put up again. These bales were thrown down from the silage pit in the winter to bed the cubicles on both sides. Hard work in the summer making easy work during the winter.

Several years later we bought an elevator that fixed to the tractor. This would pick up a row of bales in the field and drop them on the trailer. My grandfather drove this. One row of bales seemed like time wasting to him, so he would zig zag across the field trying to pick up three rows at a time. It worked until he drove over a bale or picked one up sideways. More haste, less speed came to mind.

In the mid- eighties, round balers were starting to appear. Making large four-foot bales. One bale holding as much straw as ten small bales. One man could clear a field in very little time without breaking sweat. Most cubicles are now bedded with sand, so no longer any need to cover the silage pit with thousands of small bales. Many farms now have bale choppers that will take a big bale and blow the straw into cattle pens, again negating even more of the physical work on the farms.

For our extended family, the day would end in those days as darkness fell and we would troop in for supper, discuss the day and make tentative plans for the next day. Uncles, workmen and cousins together. I think that camaraderie is the thing I most miss from that time along with aching muscles, bone weary tiredness, but already waiting for the next day and all it would bring.

Wild Oats

In the Harvest Hymn, Come, ye thankful People Come, there are two lines that resonate with me.

Wheat and Tares together sown,

Unto joy or sorrow grown.

In our fields, it was barley and wild oats. The sorrowful part was hand rogueing the wild oats. A tedious job that I detested. It was a matter of timing. We needed the barley to be nearly ripe, and the wild oats still green. The oats would grow in patches across the field and if left would ruin the sample of barley, making it less saleable and it would multiply greatly by the following year, creating an even bigger problem.

Usually, when hand rogueing, the wind would be blowing, making the barley sway in waves and creating feelings of nausea in my stomach. I am not sure if it was seasickness or vertigo. Either way, it was not pleasant. If the job was being done on a sunny day, the barley would reflect the sun into my eyes, causing me to squint.

I would work my way across the field, a strip at a time, pulling the plants out by the roots and stuffing them into a bag. I would think I had done a good job, only to turn around at the end of the strip and see other patches that I had not seen on my first sweep. When finished the bags of wild oats were then burnt, that was the only pleasure in the job. A tedious, mind numbing, thankless task that I was always glad to finish.

A barley grain is full of goodness. I would get a few heads of barley and rub them between my palms and then blow the chaff away. This would see if the crop would thrash properly when going through the combine. Then I would bite a grain in half to see if it was ripe. When ripe it will crack in half between your teeth. If not ripe, the grain is spongy when you bite into it.

The wild oat grain, by contrast, has no goodness in it. It is all husk, no feed value what so ever. But to me it is a fascinating plant. Although it looks so useless and wisht, each grain has a whisker growing out of one end. This whisker has one purpose. If the grain gets damp, the whisker will start to turn, causing the grain to move along the ground, looking for a crack in the soil to fall into. This will happen within a couple of seconds of the grain getting damp. It is my favourite party trick. Putting a wild oat grain in the palm of my hand, spitting on it (other liquids are available!) and then watching the grain crawl across my hand.

Nature at its most fascinating.

Making hay

Although in the mid 1970s, silage was starting to be made in our local area, we made all our winter feed as hay. It was usually late May or early June, that a weather window appeared and the forecast looked good for a week or so. We would cut a field each day to try and spread the work involved in carrying the hay. The next few days were spent turning and tedding the hay, trying to get it dry enough to bale. Drying grass, there is not a smell like it, beautiful. After three or four days the grass was deemed as dry enough to bale and after the dew had lifted, the baler would start to work. Small bales at the time.

We did not carry hay on trailers, but on buckrakes. These buckrakes had been adapted to fit on tractors and between our farms, we had four. Four of us youngsters would go out into the hay field and scrape a load of bales into a pile, load them up and take them into the yard, tip them outside the shed for the rest of the men to build away and then back into the field for another load. The object was to carry as many bales as possible without losing the load. If we were a bit sharp with the clutch, the tractor would rear up and drop the bales on the floor, causing unnecessary extra work.

Sometimes it would be a matter of steering the tractor into the yard with the independent brakes, as the tractor was so light on the front. I can remember as a small boy being put to sit on the bonnet of the tractor to add a bit of weight to the front and to help stop it bucking. It was a matter of continuing with the buckrakes until the field was clear of bales and then help with stacking the many bales still outside the shed, until the job was done.

Sometimes we would bale the hay too quickly. It might have been that the weather was changing or just lack of patience. Either way, the hay in the shed would start to heat up and sweat. Toadstools would start growing on the bales because of the ideal hot and humid conditions. Unfortunately, sometimes hay in that condition will spontaneously combust and the whole shed-full of hay burn.

We never actually had that happen but it was not for the lack of trying on our part, as many times, lack of patience made us bale the hay too quickly. I can remember one day in September 1977 we had to move one bay of hay and restack it in the next bay to allow the hay to breathe and cool down. It was the tenth birthday of Radio 1 and they were playing the best records from the previous ten years. We had the radio on all day keeping us company.

With our hay, we usually filled the two sheds nearest the cows- house first, then stored the rest in the big shed. During the winter, the first two sheds were replenished from the big shed on Saturdays to keep it handy for the cows. Unfortunately, if the hay was baled too quickly it was not good quality and would be cakey and full of mould. Not good for man or beast.

One of my mother's brothers, Uncle Kenneth, experimented with barn dried hay. This was supposed to be of superior quality to normal hay. It was baled green, put into the shed and then air was blown through the hay through vents to keep it cool. I hope you can see the biggest problem with this system!

The bales weighed like lead!

I was called to help carry hay along with my brother and cousin. We loaded up a buckrake on the back of a Fordson

Major and lifted the hydraulics but the tractor would not lift the weight. We had to get our hands under the buckrake and help lift it off the floor. Added to this, because the bales were so heavy, the baler twine cut into our hands making our hands sore for days.

Aaaaah, Good times!

The Accident

When I was nine years old, my father was killed in a tractor accident!

Just writing that has made me anxious.

May 20th 1968. A Monday like any other. The four of us older children had been to school as usual. Our youngest sister, Mary, was a month old that day and my mother wanted to weigh her to make sure she was 'doing'. As my gran had a large scale, we drove to Withan after school to weigh her. When we reached Withan, my gran and auntie were quite agitated and told Mother that there had been an accident at Trewothack.

My Mother turned white, "where's Brian?", she said, "where's Brian?"

Mother and auntie drove off and we were left mooching around wondering if anyone had been hurt. My Aunt returned, gathered us together and told us that our dad had been in the accident and we would probably never see him again. Fourteen words that smashed our lives and nothing would ever be the same again. We returned to Trewothack later that evening, hugged mother and we all cried. Most of the extended family came to Trewothack that evening to try and give support. Dr Dean, our family doctor came, He kissed my mother, which I thought was a bit odd at the time.

My Father had been working on a hill, trying to get rid of gorse and small trees. Apparently, the buckrake he had been using had caught in a root, causing the tractor to rear up and end up on its side. My brother Chris, who was eight at the time, and I, walked out to look at the tractor the next day. It was still on its side, with the silencer bent at right angles across the bonnet. It is that silencer that has always stuck with me. Bent and broken. It seemed to encompass everything that had happened.

In the days that followed, many friends and relations visited Mother and it seemed that many liked to tell me that I was the man of the house now and I must look after my mother. This pushed my already sky-high anxiety levels up another level, at the same time as I was trying to assimilate my own feelings of grief and trying to look after my younger brother and sisters. What I could not deal with was people visiting and starting to cry and setting everyone off. In my world, children were supposed to cry, adults were not. More anxiety.

I do not remember crying much. My own grief was not spikes of overwhelming sadness followed by periods of calm. It was more a dull, infinite sadness that always seemed to be with me. My salvation was St Anthony lighthouse. Our bedroom at Trewothack was on the third floor and from the window was a view over Falmouth Bay. My brother and I had bunk beds and I was in the top. When the perils and dangers of the night threatened to overwhelm me, I could lean out and see the light house flashing, as it had since 1835. Its presence calmed me down and cheered me up. A symbol of permanence in my uncertain world at the time.

My Father's funeral was on the Friday, us four children were hiked off out of it, taken to Helston by relations and bought a toy in the toy shop. I can remember thinking, if you think this will make everything alright, then you are sadly mistaken. I was quite resentful.

The next Monday, we went back to school and from then, until I left school seven years later, I never mentioned to anyone that my father was dead. The only teacher I told was on the day I left school. Quite shocked him, I think. My form teacher was sending out reports and asked for our father's initials. Why he could not have just put Mr Hosken, I do not know. It was a matter of going into details that I did not want to share or just telling him my father's initials. AJB. Hosken, Sir! Anxiety! Then giving Mother my report with my father's initials on. More anxiety. I was intense and introverted all through school and was glad to leave. My brother handled the situation in much the same way but hated school with a vengeance. For me, it was just something that had to be gone through.

There was no support when we returned to school. No one designated to keep an eye on us to make sure we were coping. No bereavement counselling. No Phenalgin's Friends (bereavement support for children) to help children cope with grief and come to terms with their loss.

Nothing! Just go back to school and get on with it.

The Good Old Days!

Sheaf Pitching

When I was seventeen, I had my first go at sheaf pitching. For those of you who have not seen it, sheaf pitching is a competition, where the aim is to throw a ten- pound sheaf over a bar with a two pronged pitch fork. The bar is gradually raised up to a maximum height of around thirty feet. This will usually sort the men from the boys, but if not, the competitors can move farther back from the poles until a winner is found. I found that it was something I had a natural knack for and would enter competitions whenever I had the chance.

I still get satisfaction of watching a thirty-year old body builder in a vest top, strutting out to pitch the sheaf and failing miserably, then going out myself, with my coat still on and slinging the sheaf over the bar. Small minded, I know, but still satisfying! I have done the same sort of thing at Widecombe Fair in Devon. There, they use part of a bale and throw it by hand. I have never won there, but I have made some of the locals sit up and take notice.

There are three things you need to sheaf pitch, the knack, strength and flexibility. I have the knack, the ability to get the sheaf onto the pitchfork so it is not too loose and not too tight and then to swing the pitchfork in an arc, so the sheaf flies of at just the right point and sails like a rocket up and over the bar. I am thankful to say that I still have the strength, but my flexibility, as I pass sixty, is definitely suffering.

In one of his books, James Herriot tells the story of a farm dog, whose main joy in life is chasing cars up the farm lane and off the property. In the story, he sires a litter of puppies who inherit the same tendency to chase cars. At first all is well, but as the pups get bigger and stronger and with youth on their side, the father dog finds it harder and harder to stay in the lead and it becomes a contest instead of a joy. In the end, the puppies are sold and the father dog is left, king of his domain once more.

This year, at the Young Farmers ploughing match, there was a sheaf pitching contest, as usual. I entered, as did four young Hoskens, my son and three of his cousins. Their main ambition for the evening seemed to be to beat me at sheaf pitching. Like the farm dog, I held them at bay this time, but I know, that it will not be long, before one, or all of them, with youth on their side, will beat me. When they do, I will shake their hand and congratulate them.

But not yet.

Not yet!

Mentors

I have been thinking of my mentors, the men who guided me in farming and in life. Obviously, in an ideal world, my father would have been there to guide us through the pitfalls of youth, but that was not to be! We had to rely on both my grandfathers and my uncles, all farmers, as they tried to instil their experiences and practical knowledge into our lives. I try and remember their sayings:

They think the sun shines out of his ass!

He is Holier than Thou!

One hill never speaks well of another!

Good job wild cows got short horns!

All his ducks are geese!

They think the sun rises and sets on him!

You are enough to try the patience of Job!

You are going around like the wandering tribe of Manassah!

Dear Lord, give me strength.

You put them out now and you will have five mouths grazing!

He is as old as Methusalah.

One boy is a good boy, two boys are half a boy and three boys are no good at all!

The best fertiliser is a farmer's boot!

Never turn soil downhill!

Make sure they have got four legs and a tail!

Hold on to the cow's tail and she will pull you through!

That is a shitty habit!

Obviously, these expressions of frustrations were never used about me, but I remember hearing them!

My mind takes me back to when I was twelve. Grandpa Hosken had shut Floss in the dog's house and she was frantically scratching at the door. I opened the door to see what was the matter with her and she was gone, between my legs and off. Nature calling her.

Grandpa was very annoyed.

Two months later and nature had taken its course! Floss had half a dozen squealing black and white puppies that she was nursing. A week later, grandpa came around the corner with the 12-bore shotgun in his hand, "I have shot those puppies, they are in the orchard, now you go and bury them!"

I got the shovel and went out to the orchard. The puppies were in a small lifeless pile with little spots of red all over them. I dug a pit and buried them with a tear in my eye, instinctively knowing why I was given the job. A hard lesson in life. I cannot see me doing the same to my grandsons but we live in different days.

At that time, it was acceptable to put kittens in a hessian sack and drown them, as long as it was done before their eyes were open. The alternative was a lot of mangy cats, getting more and more inbred, until they caught cat flu and died. Grandpa would shoot some of those mangy cats, but never seemed to think it might be better to do it when none of his grand children were around.

He was the seventh of ten children, in the early 1900s, when he was a small boy, his family had moved from Trevorrian Farm, St Buryan, where his family had farmed for generations to Treleage Farm and then Tregarne Farm, St Keverne.

He then moved to Clowance farm at Praze, where he farmed with several of his siblings. They milked a fairly large dairy herd at the time and had a milk round in Camborne. One of grandpa's brothers was an alcoholic and he was the one sent to pick up the money from the milk round every week, which was obviously a recipe for disaster, as the money never reached the farm. I always wonder why one of the other brothers did not go to collect the money and remove the temptation.

Grandpa then moved to Boundis Farm at Mabe before buying Withan and moving to St Martin in 1953. He could not have known that in the next five years, three of his offspring would have married a Jenkin from the adjoining farm. Both strong Methodist, farming families, with a footpath across a mere three fields dividing them. Twelve children were the result of those three marriages. All half Hosken and half Jenkin. A good mix? I could not possibly comment!

Grandpa and Gran Hosken had fifteen grandchildren in total, grandpa carried a photo of us all to show to the friends he visited if they did not show enough interest in us. He would knock them off his visiting list!

When I was in my late teens, grandpa would say to me,

"You know that girl Pierce up St Keverne (names have been changed to protect the innocent and I cannot remember the name anyway.) Why don't you ring her up and take her out for a drive?"

"BECAUSE, I don't want to."

"She is a lovely girl and she respects the Sabbath!"

"I still do not want to!"

"Humph."

Several years later it was a different story

"Did you see your girlfriend last night?"

"Yes."

"Was she pleased to see you?"

"Yes."

"Did she show you she was pleased?"

How do you answer that?

If I was reading a book when I was young, which I did a lot. Grandpa thought that was a complete waste of time and I ought to have been out working. What he would have thought of me writing one, I dread to think. Probably quietly proud. I hope so, anyway.

While farming at Withan, grandpa Hosken had a visit from a neighbour, Monty Johns. Unfortunately, grandpa did not have time to stop and speak to Mr Johns, which was a shame, as Mr Johns was selling his land, some of which was across the road from Withan entrance. Mr Johns then went to Mudgeon and agreed to sell his land to grandpa Jenkin. Which is why, to this day, my cousin Philip farms the land across from our entrance. A life lesson to everyone!

Grandpa Hosken was a kind man in many ways and good to his sisters when they had trouble in their lives, but unsentimental. He must have been about the age I am now when his eldest son was killed. He was the one who identified the body and he then spent another seven years of his life milking the cows and helping my mother, to give Chris and I the chance to farm at Withan, for which we will always be grateful.

My grandfather Jenkin's father was a miner. He was called Athansius Jenkin (what a name, knocks Brindley Hosken into a cocked hat!). He started working at the mine when he was eight years old and every day would walk two miles from his home at Boquio, up over Blackrock and onto Troon. A two- mile trek, morning and evening. During his youth, the tin mines shut down and he travelled to South Africa and continued mining there.

He returned to Cornwall and having saved some money, he bought Carnebone Farm. He contracted Miners Typhus and passed away in his forties, when my grandfather was thirteen. My Grandfather was one of six, but his parents had another five children who died in infancy. Probably due to diphtheria, tuberculosis or one of the many other diseases that there was no cure for at the time.

My grandpa and gran Jenkin started farming at Higher Poleo, Praze. They started by renting it, but after a year or two it was put up for sale. They managed to borrow the money and bought it. At this time, my grandpa lost a brother who was in his early twenties and it affected him greatly mentally. He would go out to plough with the horses and my gran would go with him and walk beside him as he walked up and down the fields giving him the strength and support to carry on.

Several years later, my gran was left half of Boderluggan Farm. They managed to buy the other half and continued farming there and renting Poleo out. With three sons growing up, in 1943, they took on the tenancy of Mudgeon Farm and ten years later bought it.

This was when Trelowarren Estate was selling off its farms (it was the same time that Grandpa Hosken bought Withan). Poleo and Boderluggan were on the granite. Black thin soils with large rocks just under the surface, that would grow grass but pretty little else. Mudgeon, by contrast would grow anything. Barley, winter cauliflower and cabbages. More options.

My grandpa told Chris and I this story when we were young and as he was not coarse in any way, it stuck in our heads. He had just moved to Mudgeon and Mr Bryant, a neighbouring farmer asked if he could help with the thrashing. The thrashing machine would move from farm to farm and thrash the grain from the sheaves of corn that had been stored at harvest. This took many men to run and the neighbouring farmers would gather at each farm when the thrashing machine turned up. It was driven and pulled by a steam traction engine.

Grandpa turned up at Mr Bryant's farm and was put to pitch the sheaves onto the thrashing machine. There was grandpa and two other men. These two men were useless, either lazy or ineffectual and grandpa was left to do the bulk of the work. The local farmers were undoubtedly testing him out. At the end of the day, Mr Bryant came over, "Well Mr Jenkin, how have you got on?" My grandpa replied, "I could shit better men than those two!"

The other story concerning Thrashing happened at Tremayne Farm which joins Mudgeon on the other side. Tremayne has since been bought by my cousin, Philip and now runs with Mudgeon. Just the road side of Tremayne farm yard is the big house. In the 1930s, the owners of the big house would not let the thrashing machine travel past it. This resulted in the Traction engine and thrashing machine having to travel down the steep hill to Gent and then to travel through the woods and up by the back lane into Tremayne yard.

This must have taken an extra hour and was also extremely dangerous. There were no servo brakes at the time and there was a real danger that the engine and machine would run away on the hill. This situation must have really wound up the farmers and engine drivers involved. The matter was apparently resolved when the tenant of Tremayne threatened to quit their tenancy and leave the farm. At the time, farms were almost impossible to let and the owners capitulated and let the thrashing machine and engine enter by the main entrance.

My uncle Geoffrey Hosken and my uncle Ronnie Jenkin farmed near us and we worked together at harvest and hay time. They were support for my mother after my father died and advised us on farming matters. They were both superb farmers. Uncle Geoffrey had moved to Trewothack after my father's death and by luck and good judgement had managed to buy neighbouring land.

This enabled him to more than double the size of Trewothack in his working life, from 180 acres to nearly 400 acres. The luck was that the neighbouring farm was being sold off twenty or thirty acres every couple of years. This enabled him to buy it slowly without extending himself too far financially.

Uncle Ronnie had three sons and he managed to pass on a farm to each of them. He farmed Mudgeon and bought Treworgie in 1975 and then Higher Trenower in 1988. Although they were both superb farmers, they had different ways of looking at things and if one said buy, the other would say sell. After we left school and trying to take what they both said on board was extremely difficult. We could not do right for doing wrong. In the end my mother had to tell them that we needed to be left alone to do what we thought was right. This eased the pressure somewhat.

They have all passed on now, along with my mother's other two brothers. Why did we not ask them more questions about their lives when they were alive. They farmed in the era of tractors taking the place of horses. They lived and farmed through the war. They all managed to survive, expand and prosper in farming. Would they be proud of Chris and I, or disappointed that we had not managed to achieve more in our own farming lives.

Praze A.I. Centre

During the 1960s, the Milk Marketing Board also ran a breeding programme, where they reared bulls to hopefully become the next super sires of the main dairy breeds. In those days, getting bulls to be breeding sires, was a long drawn- out affair. They needed to reach sexual maturity, sire a number of heifer calves and then wait until these heifers had calved, to discover whether they were passing on a majority of positive traits. This made a time lapse of around seven years before they became proven bulls. The process is much faster these days, D.N.A. can be taken from a couple of hairs on a day-old calves back and the traits he carries will be known almost immediately. A much quicker pay back.

In the sixties, the bulls waiting to be proven, were laid off, or kept at a site, until they were deemed to be used at stud or beefed. One such site was at Praze, the site was also used as a base for the inseminators, who travelled all over west Cornwall in their mini minors, inseminating cows on the hundreds of dairy farms that were in existence at the time.

There were around thirty bulls kept at Praze. Mainly friesians, with a few ayrshires, guernseys and Jerseys. My father's cousin was head stockman there at the time and as he had a son my age, I would sometimes stay there during the school holidays. Sometimes the bulls were indoors, either tethered or in pens and they would lower their heads and bellow as we passed by.

The Jerseys were the worst, small and vicious. The big friesians could be led by one man, but the small jerseys always had two men leading them. In the summer, they were all tethered outside, far enough apart to prevent them fighting. If we were lucky, we would travel around the field in the land rover to feed them. Their small eyes would look at us and they would scrape their heads on the floor. If the land rover got too close, they would give it a duff and put yet another dent in each panel, which would make our day. Probably, having children in a vehicle, in a field of bulls, would not be recommended in these more enlightened times.

While staying at Praze, I along with my cousin, Geoffrey, had certain opportunities that I did not have at home. We could catch a bus just outside their house, travel to Camborne and go to the cinema to watch Dr Who on the big screen. Either catching the bus back or having chips and walking back. We also climbed over some barbed wire in order to look down into a local open mine to see how deep it was. The inky black water was about eighty feet down. I shudder to think of the outcome, if we had slipped over the edge. Another time, it seemed like a good idea to sling a length of string across the main road to Camborne. What were we thinking?

Sometimes, Geoffrey's father would go fishing at St Ives and drop us off at the beach. We would walk along the quay, past the proliferation of hippies, smoking their sweet-smelling roll ups and spend the day swimming and taking turns in diving off the diving board on one of the three beaches. Left to our own devices till the fishing was finished.

The buildings at Praze are still standing, but no longer hold bulls or any form of animals. There are less inseminators these days, as there are fewer dairy farms and many farmers have been trained to artificially inseminate their cattle themselves. The inseminators no longer use the buildings at Praze as a base, but I remember the characters when they did. Michael Basher, who would get into a huff if you used a Holstein bull. Chris Vincent, who would tease you about various local girls and who died young. Danny Chinn and Mr Goldsworthy. A group of men that brought both banter and comraderies to the many isolated farms in the district, during my early life.

My Parents Farming Life

I have already written that my parents lived on adjoining farms, my father at Withan and my mother at Mudgeon. There is a public footpath joining them across three fields, The Slates Close and Bramble Field at Withan and the Higher Gobbin at Mudgeon. Quite useful for courting purposes, I should imagine. When mother and father got married in 1957, they were offered my father's aunt's farm to rent. This was Chywoone Farm at St Keverne.

They lived at Chywednack, a small cottage that had no driveway, so getting to it meant a short walk across the fields from Chywoone. They carried me, as a small baby, up across the field in a carrycot when they needed to go anywhere. This was fine in the summer, but not so well in the winter when the fields were wet. So, in the winter, they would move into Chywoone farmhouse with my great aunt.

Chywoone Farm was very wet and very rocky, not small rocks, but car size rocks. Some on the surface and some just under. It would grow grass but was not really suitable for other crops. My father had a blasting licence to use dynamite and would blow up the rocks that were most inconvenient to him. There is still one rock at Chywoone with a small hole drilled in it, ready to blast, but somehow the job never got done.

I like to see it occasionally, to remind me of father. While at Chywoone, my parents milked around twenty cows, reared pigs and father did some contracting with a mole plough, as many farms were putting in water troughs at the time and not just relying on streams and ponds for the animals to drink from. Unfortunately, their dairy herd caught brucellosis which caused contagious abortions in the cows and resulted in unthrifty cattle that would not milk, were infertile and liable to pass the disease to humans. I should think it was hard going at the time and it was the pigs that got them through the period.

Several years later, they had the chance to move to Treveador. Treveador joins Withan (don't they all!). It was farmed by my grandfather's brother. He wanted to retire, but wanted someone to take over his dairy herd rather than disperse it. So, we moved to Treveador. I think me, Chris and Anne were all born at this time. Jane was born while we were at Treveador. Father still ran Chywoone and would travel from one to the other on a motorbike with the dog sitting on the petrol tank.

Treveador was a bit like Withan being fairly slopy, but would grow broccoli (winter cauliflower) and cabbage. The broccoli was precision drilled, in early May and transplanted in July. The first job was to pull plant. This involved pulling the closely packed plant, checking they had a good root structure and did not have button hearts (an empty space between the leaves that would not develop a head). They were then tied in bunches of one hundred and taken to be transplanted.

As children, we would pull the weeds in the yard and place them in piles. We were pulling plant. Some help! Father had a four- row planter that fixed to the tractor. It had four seats, in front of the seats there was a tray to hold the plant. Under each seat were two wheels that faced each other and pressed the soil around the plant as it was planted. It also had a small wheel that would click and tell the casual workers on the planter when to drop the plant.

Before planting, the plants roots were dipped in an obnoxious chemical, to stop pests eating the roots. I would sometimes ride on the footplate of the tractor beside my father, looking back at the planted rows and at Mrs Abraham's massive bosom, as she bent forward and dropped the plants into the warm, damp soil!

As a girl, my mother helped her brother plant broccoli by hand. Uncle Ronnie would push the Cornish shovel into the soil and then push it forward, creating a slot for mother to drop the plant into. The shovel was then removed and a boot used to press the soil around the plant. Then on to the next one. I imagine the ground had been marked out beforehand to show them where to drop the plants. Broccoli were planted at 8,000 to the acre, so planting them by hand must have been a slow task.

I suppose I was eight when I did my first day's work, mending plant. They were not broken, but sometimes the planters would miss a click, either taking another handful of plant or losing concentration. This would mean a gap left in the row of plants that had to be filled by the mender. Mending involved following the planter with a trowel and handful of plant and filling any gap in a pair of rows. I mended all day and was very pleased with myself. I think my father was very pleased with me as well.

My parents had two men working for them by now. In the winter, they would go out to harvest the broccoli, with large wicker baskets on their backs. They would cut and trim the broccoli heads, then throw them in the basket. These when full were tipped into a trailer and later in the day they would all be packed into crates, labelled, then taken by lorry to Helston and loaded on the train, taken to Covent Garden before ending up on the shop shelves. Cabbage was really an insurance policy. If there was snow or severe frosts, the broccoli would get frosted and the heads would rot. The whole field would stink. No broccoli, so the price of other greens, such as cabbage would soar.

The dairy herd had expanded while we were living at Treveador. At the time, all the cows had horns, which was a nuisance. They could swing their heads around and injure farmers or farm workers and could also cause a lot of damage to other cows when they were fighting. While we were at Treveador, the vet came one day and sawed the horns off all the cows.

Probably a day's work, expensive but well worth it. The cows were confused for a time and as they breathed out, the condensation came out at the top of their heads, where their horns had been. When I was farming in my own right, if ever we had cattle that we had missed dehorning, I made sure they were removed as quickly as possible. I did not want a horn in the ribs or in anyone else's ribs either.

By the mid 1960s with the now increased dairy herd and the broccoli and cabbage, fat bullocks and pigs, my parents were doing very well financially and starting to look for a farm to buy. I know they looked at a farm near Praze, but I didn't know if there were any others.

Then Trewothack came up for sale.

The owner Mr Collins was suffering from ill health and decided to retire early. Trewothack was sold at auction, probably in the Angel Hotel in Helston, where most auctions of farms were conducted. The final bid was £36,000 and the farm was knocked down to My father and uncle. I believe that the general consensus at the time was that they would never pay for it. As children, we knew nothing about this until the deal was done.

Trewothack was and is a fantastic farm. Whereas most farms in the area were around 100 acres at the time, Trewothack was 180 acres. When you drove in the lane, Parc Tonkin was on the left, a sixteen-acre level field. Barn Parc was on the right, a twelve-acre level field. I had barely seen a level field at the time and certainly not a sixteen acre one. Then as you drove into the yard, a range of two storey traditional barns built around a courtyard, with a single level barn in the centre.

The farmhouse was three storeys high with large rooms and bay windows. On the stairs was a stag's head that remained there when we moved in. Across the yard, was the farm cottage. It had a conservatory attached that homed a large vine that produced grapes. The rest of the land mostly faced south, mainly large fields with one large orchard and two smaller ones. There were lanes snaking out to the farther fields, a great asset as it stopped dairy cattle having to cross one field to get to another.

As you drove back out the lane, over the brow, the whole vista of Falmouth Bay opens up before you. It always makes me stop and take in the beauty. I always wonder, if I still lived at Trewothack, would that view still grab me every time?

We moved to Trewothack and my father installed a milking parlour. It was a 5/10 Weycroft Macford parlour. The 5/10 meant that it had ten standings for the cows, five each side and five units that milked cows on both sides. It would be laughed at now, but back then it was state of the art. The first milking was an experience, the cows would not walk into the standings and had to be physically pushed into place. The friesians were not bad, but the guernseys were completely cussed and would not move.

As a boy of nine, I remember that milking. One man was up in the beams trying to push the cows into place. We also had a large shed erected at the same time. It was a concrete at cost shed. Around ninety foot long, with a span of fifty foot and around forty foot high. One of the men who were erecting it climbed a ladder and then walked along the six-inch concrete beam to the centre of the span to fix it with two bolts. It made my blood run cold at the time and still does today. If he had fallen, there is no doubt he would have been killed.

My father's intention was to keep on farming Treveador as well as Trewothack. I never heard what his plans were and how he was going to manage both farms. As you have read earlier in this book, my father's death brought everything to a shuddering halt. My mother was thirty-three years old, left a widow with five children under ten years old, the youngest a month old.

The cows still needed milking, the bullocks still needed feeding, there was still work to be done. Luckily, we had workmen and the family pitched in and did what they could as mother grieved and coped with her children's grief and tried to work out the best path for our family.

That year we had a large bed of broccoli plant at Trewothack and as we were not going to plant broccoli, they were sold to various farmers in the district. Chris and I pulled some of them. One man bought some plant and then kept mother waiting for the money. A pretty lowdown trick, considering the position we were in at the time.

Undoubtably, my father would have liked us to have stayed at Trewothack, but it was just not feasible. Trewothack was too big for mother to manage, with five children under ten years to look after. Eventually, mother sold her half of Trewothack to my grandfather and bought Withan from him. This was all done by auctioneer's valuation. We then had a farm sale and sold most of the cows, leaving twenty to move to Withan with us.

Most of the farm machinery was sold as well, along with the machinery that my father had made. A dung spreader, a post hole borer, an auger for drilling holes through hedges and a grain blower. He never passed that skill onto me and I struggle to weld two bits of metal together. We moved to Withan, no more looking out the window at the lighthouse, no more sixteen-acre fields, no more milking parlour, no more 180 acres!

Withan was 100 acres with steep hills on one side and very steep hills on the other side. It was described to me once by a neighbour, Bill Bryant (son of previously mentioned Mr Bryant) as the worst farm in the parish. I was just glad he did not say worst farmed! I could not disagree with him. I am sure that many of my farming neighbours would like to add Withan to their portfolio of land, but I never heard any of them say they would like to farm it in its own right.

On the plus side, Withan farmhouse is a picturesque long house that could be split into two separate houses. It is separate from and on the other side of the lane from the farm buildings. Unlike most farmhouses, as you drive down the lane, you come to the front, white washed side of the house and not the back. Ever since Grandpa bought Withan, if two generations were not living in it, then half the house was let out for self- catering visitors or Bed and Breakfast visitors. Thankfully, the house sells itself to visitors.

Withan runs down to Frenchman's Creek (made famous by Daphne Du Maurier's book of the same name). The Creek is a lovely peaceful spot, tree laden and beautiful. Better when the tide is in, but you cannot have everything. There are also ten acres of ancient woodland bordering the hills. Because of how mild the climate is, sycamores grow like weeds and need to be kept in check. If left idle for several years, the place would soon grow in.

My grandpa and gran stayed at Withan and helped mother run the dairy herd, with help from my uncles until Chris and I left school some seven years later.

Secondary School

September 1970, I started secondary school at Penrose Road Secondary Modern School, having failed my eleven plus. The rite of passage that allowed me to wear long trousers to school for the first time. The school may have been secondary, but it certainly was not modern. Built around 1900, it was in a bit of a state, even fifty years ago. The rat hole that was the boy's toilets, open to the elements and used by the fourth years as a smoking den. Best avoided, if possible. Just down the road from the school was a tobacconist shop, with four vending machines selling cigarettes outside.

Ideally placed, where pupils could buy their fags without going into the shop, before school or sneaking out during break. It seemed likely that the staff used the same shop. If I ever had the need to visit the staff room, the door would be opened and it was impossible to see across the room because of the thick smoke that permeated around it. Just down from the school was the drill hall that we used for P.E. It is now part of Helston Museum. At the time I was in school, Helston Fatstock Show was held in the drill hall, on the third Monday of November, around my birthday.

We would visit the show from school and see all the cattle tied up and sweating, immaculately turned out to try and catch the judge's eye. Straw covering all the floor and at one end, the vegetables on display, broccoli, flatpole cabbage, mangolds, turnips and samples of barley, wheat and hay. All there to be judged. I believe there were cookery classes as well, but these were situated in the guild hall and at the time we did not have time to visit the guildhall as well.

P.E. at the drill hall was with Mr Hosking. Old School! Did not take prisoners! For example, two boys scuffing. "Alright lads, form a ring! You two wanted to fight, now fight!" One ended up crying and then it was on with the lesson. Another time the whole class had annoyed him. There were heavy wooden benches surrounding the hall. "Alright lads, eight to a bench, up above your heads. Now run around the hall. We were running around till exhaustion took over. His left trainer, he used as a cane.

A boy across his knee and a couple of slaps with his trainer across the backside soon restored order. Once I had a bad ankle. I had scraped it on a hedge when cycling home and it had turned nasty. I did not have a note to escape P.E. I said to Mr Hosking, "I am sorry Sir, but I have hurt my ankle and don't think I should do cross country".

He looked at me, "that's alright my boy. I know you wouldn't skive!"

Penrose Road had about 300 pupils, mostly from the rural villages on the Lizard Peninsula, among them, Farmer's son's and Fishermen's sons. Mainly going through the motions until they could leave school and get on with some useful work. The teachers were mainly alright, with one or two useless ones that had no control over any class. A couple of teachers would use corporal punishment, but not very often and I was never hit.

After two years at Penrose Road, the three Helston schools, Penrose Road, Gwealhellis and the Grammar school amalgamated into a comprehensive school with 1700 pupils. I walked into my class at the beginning of the third year and wondered why there were men in my form. Some of them were very well developed. When we had games, there was one boy in my class who would stroll around the changing room naked, flicking his pride and joy as he went! This was very intimidating to someone like me, who was still singing soprano at the time and barely had a pride, never mind a joy!

On the whole, the teachers were alright, with one or two vicious sods. One boy in my form was slapped so hard, it knocked him to the ground. Fifty years ago, and I remember it as if it was yesterday. Our own form teacher was a man that would go from a normal man to a raging shaking lunatic in thirty seconds for no discernible reason. I ought to have told him to calm down! Or perhaps not. Blackboard rubbers were used as missiles by some teachers and hurled across the room at errant pupils.

I was in the top groups for English and Maths and it took a lot of work to stay there, but I thought I ought to try, for the honour of Penrose Road. We were far behind the other two schools academically. One of my English teachers asked me, "can't you use longer words in your essays?" Little did she know the erudite, meticulous, philosophical, pertinacious person I would become. I think she would have been very surprised, that one day, I would right a book!

We were very fortunate at Helston School when Two teachers started a school Young Farmers Club. We would meet on Monday dinner breaks and have speakers come to teach us dairy and beef stock judging. I was elected the first

Chairman of the club, which involved introducing the speaker and closing the meeting. Four of us went to YFC competitions day and won the points judging competition. In 1974, Princess Anne was attending the YFC County Rally, she was meeting a representative of every club in the County and then having lunch with them.

I was asked to go and represent Helston School YFC. I met Princess Anne and then into the marque for lunch. I was sat next to the Bishop of Truro and we had lobster for lunch. Quite intimidating, sat next to a Bishop as I tried to work out how to eat a lobster. First and last time I have ever had it. I suppose it taught me to make the most of the opportunities that were presented to me.

In the last six months of my school life, my grandfather fell ill and for a time it seemed that I may have had to leave school before taking my exams. Thankfully this did not happen, as I had worked hard to be in a position to take my O levels

I left school on 20th June 1975, without a backward look, ready to get on with my farming.

Mother

I am writing this piece twelve months to the day that my mother passed away, as I try to do justice to her memory and the special woman that she was. As you will already have read, she was widowed at thirty- three and left with five children under ten, the youngest a month old. She had to be both father and mother to us, so we did not get away with much. Mother had an edge in her voice that would cut glass and when she spoke to us in that tone, we knew she meant business and we had better back off.

She also had a look that conveyed the same message. She controlled us by will power. I can remember being smacked once; this was for fighting with Chris when I was about fifteen. We were always scuffing, but this time it got a bit more serious and she slapped my upper arm with some vigour. Years later she explained that as we were getting older, she needed to be able to control us and this was the way of telling us that she was still the boss. As if we needed reminding.

After we had moved to Withan, Mother would help Grandpa with the milking in the mornings. Our job was to make our beds and then make and have breakfast, so we were ready to go to school when she came in from milking. At that time, she was up before six every day and still grieving for my father. I would wake up and hear her breaking her heart in the next bedroom and go back to sleep, so sad that I was powerless to help her through her grief.

Mother brought us up in a strict Methodist home, with shades of the Temperance Society and the Band of Hope. There was absolutely no alcohol in the house. I remember as a teenager, being at a friend's house, when the Vicar called. My friend's parents offered him a beer. I was absolutely gob smacked!

Firstly, they had the Demon Drink in the house!

Secondly, they offered it to a Minister of the cloth!

Thirdly, he drank one!

The whole situation was completely alien to me at the time.

Although the farm took a lot of her time, Mother tried to make sure that we did not miss out more than was possible. She would take us to Gillan or St Anthony swimming in the summer holidays or up to the swimming pool at St Martin school. My sister Anne's birthday was on August 4th and on that day, we often went to Maenporth or Poldhu beach along with many of our cousins. Every September we had a week's holiday. We usually went with another family and did not go any farther than Devon. Usually, a week on Dartmoor or Exmoor or even North Cornwall. Just a change of scenery and a chance for Mother to be Mum and not farmer for a week. Good memories.

My Mother was a very positive person and although it would have been easy to sink into depression and self- pity, she never did. Her cup was always half full. Withan was pretty much an ideal place to view the solar eclipse in 1999. The day came and the sky clouded over. The sky went dark and we could see hundreds of camera flashes across the Helford River, but we could not see the sun. At St Martin, a mile away, the clouds cleared and they saw the diamond ring! As we walked in afterwards, I said, "I have waited thirty years to see that and we saw absolutely nothing!"

Mother said, "I think we were very lucky to see that!"

I replied, "your cup is always half full, never half empty!"

"Yes, and your life will be a lot happier if you look at life in the same way!"

That told me and to be honest, feeling slightly ashamed, I took her advice on board for the future.

After Chris and I left school, Mother was able to take more of a back seat with the farming and ease up on the work. In the next couple of decades, all five of us got married and fifteen grandchildren appeared on the scene. Mother was still living at Withan, she had moved into a small barn on the farm, all on one level, with central heating and just big enough for her to manage. We were living in the farmhouse, so she saw a lot of our three as they were growing up and eventually having children of their own.

In her sixties, Mother developed thyroid cancer. This was successfully treated but the treatment interfered with her vocal cords and resulted in her losing all the strength in her voice and having to speak in a whisper. No sooner had Mother got over Thyroid cancer, she developed breast cancer, which was completely unrelated. This was successfully treated as well with a mastectomy. For several years after the cancer's she was relatively healthy until her heart started playing up.

She then had open heart surgery to replace a valve and several stents were put in. After that, she said that she would have no more operations. The heart operation had been hard on her body and she struggled to stand upright. Several years later there was a suggestion that the thyroid cancer was coming back. "Well," she said, "if this is it, I have had a good life!"

I thought, "maybe you have, but it could have been a damn sight better!"

Last autumn, the thyroid cancer did return and it was incurable. In her last few months all five of us were able to spend time with her and help with her care. The nurses were coming to visit her every day. She was able to continue living in her home and made plans for her own funeral, as she gradually got weaker. On Christmas Day she could not swallow the pain killers any longer and had a driver fitted. She passed away peacefully on 29th December 2019, with all five of her children around her bed. When all is said and done, who could ask for more.

Mother's funeral was held a fortnight later at Manaccan Chapel, the chapel where she had worshipped for more than fifty years. Around 250 attended, many who came back to Withan afterwards. We are all thankful that Mother did not have to live through this year of Covid, with my sisters not being allowed to visit and funerals limited to thirty people and all the stress that would have gone with it.

We had many letters from people, who's lives Mother had touched, many of them very moving and saying what Mother had meant to them. In all my sixty- two years, I never lived more than fifty yards from my mother. I know a couple of times in her life, I did not give her the emotional support that she needed, but I hope I was a good son to her.

No Regrets!

After Dinner Speaking

When I was a Young Farmer, I would sometimes enter Speaking competitions. There would be preliminary rounds, then a county final and you could progress to South West, Southern and then the National Final. Our team would quite often get to the County finals, but I did not have the talent to go farther. There were several speaking competitions. Junior public speaking, where all the team were under sixteen. One member was the Chairman, who had to chair the meeting, introduce the speaker and close the meeting.

Another member was the speaker, he or she could choose the subject they wished to speak on. It may have been a hobby, or their family farm, or anything else that interested them. The third member of the team had to ask a relevant question to the speaker and then propose the vote of thanks. My daughter, Sarah, her now husband Alan and her friend Katie, entered this competition and went on to win the national final. (Just thought I would throw that in.)

Another speaking competition is Brains Trust. In this competition, there is a chairman and three panellists. The Chairman is given a series of topics and has to pick three for the panel to discuss. The panel have no idea what the subjects are that they are going to be discussing, which is where the skill lies, being able to talk off the cuff and hopefully make sense.

The third competition is debating. Self-explanatory and dull. At least to me.

The fourth speaking competition is After Dinner Speaking. My favourite! The team are given a dinner to speak at. It could be

"The Master Butchers Society."

"The Association of Travel Agents."
"The National School Teachers Association."
"The Allotment Society."
"The Dog Breeders Society."

These are all examples that have been used in the past. The team consists of a chairman, the speaker, who proposes the toast, the responder to the speaker, the proposer of the toast to the guests, and the responder to that toast.

Although I never made it in speaking competitions beyond the County final, I have been quite successful in helping to train the present Young Farmers in public speaking. Getting to the Southern Finals with one after Dinner Speaking team and missing out on the National Finals by a whisker. That team did have my daughter, son in law and nephew as part of it. Basking in reflected glory!

The art of training the team in After Dinner Speaking was to give all the speakers a very different persona. For example, if all four speakers at, "The National School Teachers Association", decided to be teachers, it would be difficult for the judges to differentiate between them and could be boring.

One Dinner was, "The Preservation of African Wildlife Society". It would have been easy for every speaker to condemn big game hunters. We turned it around, the main speaker argued that big game hunting gave the animals a monetary value and as they had a value, they would not be killed out of hand by the local population. I was very pleased with that theory and it certainly differentiated our speaker from the rest of the speakers at that dinner.

All of the speakers in our teams had different skills. Some just give off an air of authority, some can take on a character and become that character, some can give a speech with no notes and some are natural chairman, who have the ability to relax the other speakers.

Training the Brains Trust took a different skill set. The Brain Trust team were mainly under twenty-one years of age and this competition was quite often their first try at public speaking. Once we had picked a chairman, it was a matter of thinking up relevant current topics that were likely to be on the list, getting the panellists to discuss them and to look for tangents that would expand the subject. This was also a skill that the chairman needed.

If the panel dried up, the chairman needed to take them in another direction and discuss the topic from another angle. A good chairman could carry a poor panel, but a good panel could not carry a poor chairman. It was also necessary to stop the panellists from picking up bad habits, "fer to…ummm eeeer" as their minds raced, thinking of something relevant to say. We always told the chairman to repeat the subject being discussed, to give the panellists a little more thinking time.

Public Speaking is a necessary life skill that we all need at some point in our lives, I will always be grateful to the men who gave me the ability to speak in public and trained me in the art. I hope the Young Farmers that I have helped train, will one day look back with affection at that time in their lives and remember the nerves before the competitions and the euphoria afterwards, especially if they progressed to the next stage in the competition.

Allotments

The Allotment Society was a subject that came up during a After Dinner Speaking competition. Two members of our team had to speak at the Allotment Society Dinner. As the trainer, I did some research on allotments and was amazed at the complexity of them. I always thought an allotment was a bit of land that a person rented to grow vegetables. End of story.

These days, land is measured in hectares. 100 metres by 100 metres. 10,000 square metres. A hectare is roughly 2.5 acres. I work in acres. I have always worked in acres. I can visualise an acre.! I cannot visualise a hectare. There is no soul in a hectare. I am a small-minded luddite, resisting progress!

I know that imperial measurements seem to have no rhyme or reason but there is logic in them.

A furlong or furrow length is 220 yards long. This was the length of ground, a team of oxen, could pull a plough in the 1300s without stopping for a rest.

A chain is 22 yards long. A chain by a furlong is an acre and is the area of ground a team of oxen could plough in a day.

A rod is 5.5 yards and is a quarter of a chain.

The actual size of an allotment is 1 rod by 10 rods. Or one quarter of a chain by one quarter of a furlong. This means that sixteen allotments would fit perfectly in an acre of ground. How organised is that? This area of ground was big enough for a family to grow enough vegetable to live on for twelve months of the year. Presumably, it was called an allotment as each family was allotted that amount of ground for their own use. Joined up thinking. A system where there was order. Maybe in the present day, we could learn something from our past!

Withan

After my grandfather moved to Withan in 1953, he widened the entrance to the farm and built two gate posts that were painted white. Those two posts are still there, despite the attentions of various trailers and lorries, nudging them over the years. The original gate rusted out and was replaced by a galvanised gate, still with scrolls welded on, to differentiate it from a normal farm gate. The farm lane, originally tarmacked, with deep pot holes at random points, has been concreted.

The lane itself, some 500 yards in length still starts level, before sloping away, all the way to the bottom of the yard. As youngsters we were always looking to buy or scrounge pram wheels to make go karts and race down the lane, struggling to make the corner, half way down. Sometimes coming to grief, but it did not stop us, a few tears, then on again.

When we moved to Withan in 1968, there was an old Jones self- propelled baler parked on the verge of the lane, rusting into obsolescence. It still had the driver's platform, so we would clamber up and pretend to drive it. Around the last corner and the Farmhouse still comes in sight. A long house, with a wing at the far end, whitewashed and framed by sycamore trees, with roses still growing over the front door. It has been modernised over the last fifty years, firstly by my mother, then Ruth and I, finally by David and his wife, Beth.

There is a new slate roof, the old roof replaced after the wood pins holding the slates on rotted out. The old, damp, cold wing sitting room now has a woodburning stove fitted, which helps to keep it warm and dry. The other sitting room had the fireplace pulled out by us, revealing a large inglenook, with an enormous oak beam holding the chimney in place. (Thankfully). There is now another woodburning stove in the inglenook, keeping that room warm and dry. The house is over 300 years old and is still earning its keep with our self-catering visitors.

On the other side of the lane is the farm yard. The single storey brick-built barn, with the small ventilation shaft built on top is largely the same as it was when the Trenerry's had their photograph taken in front of it nearly a hundred years ago. The only difference being the large galvanised door that Chris and I had fitted, to enable us to clean it out with a tractor. The two- storey barn is virtually the same as it was fifty years ago, apart from new doors.

Across from these barns are the small buildings that Grandpa kept turkeys in. They are now full of firewood. The old two storied cob barn is still standing. The ground floor used to hold pigs, the top storey with its rotting floor and missing planks, was used by us as a Laboratory. We used to make up concoctions of rotten eggs and wild garlic plants and store them in small animal medicine bottles. They were a lovely shade of green and stank to high heaven.

Beside the cob barn was an old army, asbestos, nissen hut. This hut also held pigs originally. When we moved to Withan, we used it for cattle, but eventually we replaced it, as the cattle were smashing the asbestos as they tried to jump through it. The single storey barn was used as a cow's house and there were standings for twenty cows. The other cow's house, attached to it, held fourteen cows.

On the other side of the cow's house was the Mowey. The Mowey had apple trees growing on it, my grandpa's bee hives, a few hens and gooseberry bushes. On the hedge between the Mowey and the Four acre were a line of massive Elm trees. Years ago, they succumbed to Dutch Elm Disease and were cut down for firewood. Elms still try and grow at Withan, but they get to a certain height and then get the disease and die.

The Mowey was also used as a dumping ground and there were two lorry cabs left there. The backs of them probably turned into trailers. We could get into the lorries and pretend we were driving to market. There was also a caravan parked in the Mowey in which we sometimes slept in the summer. It had a wind- up record player inside, but only one record, "In a Persian Market". The apple trees in the Mowey were moved when we erected the cubicle house, along with the lorry cabs and caravan.

Fifty years ago, the cows walked between the back door of the house and the lawn to get to the field behind the house. We eventually diverted the cows around the back, so they did not need to pass the house. The cows originally drank from streams or the pond, part way up the lane. These were then gradually upgraded to baths in each field. I eventually, as we milked more cows, upgraded until we had a concrete 400-

gallon water trough in each field. The field gates were also widened over the last fifty years.

From wooden ten- foot gates to galvanised twelve to fifteen- foot gates. I still get pleasure in having all my gates hanging and latching. We still have one gate that my uncle made out of an old hay rake. It has the two massive cast iron wheels welded into the centre and the curved metal of the rakes making intricate patterns around the outside. I lengthened this gate some years ago to create a wider gateway, but I am loath to replace it. It is part of the history of Withan and has been hung on the same gatepost for more than fifty years.

Originally, grandpa had dug a well in Higher Calanchard for water. This was six feet deep and had a diameter of a yard. The water ran through pipes all over the farm by gravity, as Higher Calanchard was the highest field on the farm. Chris and I dug the well deeper and wider and it worked well, until we had a prolonged dry spell, when it would dry up. We eventually drilled a borehole for water, which has not ever dried up. The bore hole is in Higher Calanchard as well. Amazing that the most water is found in our highest field. 250 feet above sea level!

The fields at Withan have barely altered in the last fifty years. We have not taken out any hedges, not because I am holier than thou, but because I could not see that there would be any advantage or efficiency in so doing. The field behind the house (I really must find out its proper name) is the one field that has had most altering. It was a wet field that had a deep droke down across it, with a wet woody patch part way across it and wet boggy patches, where we got well and truly stuck with the tractor.

We piped the droke, drained the wet patches and cleared the wet woody patch, making a much more usable field. (It does not necessarily make me a bad person!)

We have two fields in which the hills are fenced off. Around 800 yards of fences. I planted trees along these fences. First, we put a strip of plastic to keep the weeds down, then slit a hole and planted saplings, around two feet high into the soil. A double row of Hawthorn, Blackthorn, Field Maple, Wild Rose and various other Hedgerow plants.

Over three thousand trees in total. The next few years, we had to keep weeding them. Now, twenty years later, we have a stock proof hedge, around ten feet tall and the biggest problem is to stop the trees getting any taller. I have therefore in my lifetime planted more hedges than I have taken out. You never hear that from the ranters and ravers who spend their lives castigating farmers on their evil practises.

Leaving School

I left school on 20th June 1975, after taking my O levels. grandpa was by now over seventy and his health was deteriorating. It was time for him to ease back on the work, let me, and a year later Chris as well, take it on. During our time at school, Uncle Ronnie had been farming half of Withan. When I left school, we took it all in hand. We were milking twenty cows at the time. They were tied up in the cow's house to be milked, by a chain around their neck. We had three bucket units to milk them.

You had to squeeze between two cows, plug the unit into the vacuum line and attach the unit to the cow. Then onto the next stall with the second unit and then the third. By then, the first cow was finished and the unit could be taken off and placed on the second cow in the stall. Remembering to empty the bucket first. The bucket of milk was emptied into a large container sitting on the milk churn. This container had a paper filter at the bottom, the milk would be filtered through, into the milk churn.

When the churn was full, the cooler was placed into it. The cooler had a paddle that would rotate when water was run through it. The water also flowed through the paddle and gradually cooled the milk. There was a passage way in front of the cows and this was used to drop some cows cake into the cow's troughs as they were being milked.

Each cow had her own stall and as they came in from the field, would find their own particular stall and wait to be tied in. Most cows were no trouble, but some would squeeze together as you tried to get between them and lean on you, to make life difficult. The odd cow might lift her leg and give you a small kick for fun, or cough as you walked past and spatter shit all over you. During the summer, the cows only came in for milking and then went back out to grass.

During the winter, they were tied up for most of the time and fed hay in their troughs. The hay was stored close by and it was a simple matter to break the bale into chunks and give a chunk to each cow. Each stall had a water trough to enable each cow to drink. During the winter, we had to go out last thing and, "tend up". This involved going into the cow's house, which was lovely and warm with all the cows inside, then giving any cow that needed it another chunk of hay and making sure their water troughs were clean.

Then throwing a bit more straw underneath them to make a comfortable bed for them to lie on and then into our own beds. We also grew kale for the cows to strip graze in the winter. While they were out grazing kale, we had time to clean the muck out of the cow's houses. Both cow's houses could be scraped out by tractor, we were always taught that if we could not get into a shed with a tractor, then alter it until we could! As Withan has quite wet heavy soil, the kale field would be very muddy and sometimes it was a struggle to walk out and move the electric fence, that rationed how much kale the cows had each day.

The muddy conditions sometimes affected the cows and they would get an infection in their feet. At the time, this was treated by warming up kaolin poultice, this was then placed on the cow's foot and wrapped in a bandage. This treatment would draw the poison out of the cow's foot and hopefully cure the problem. The muddy kale fields also made the cows udders very dirty as they came in to be milked and made work, as we tried to get them clean enough to be milked.

The full milk churns were labelled with our name and dropped onto the milk stand. This was a platform at the same hight as the milk lorry. The milk lorry would drive alongside the milk stand and it was a simple matter to transfer the full churns onto the lorry and leave empty churns in their place.

Many of the fields at Withan border the woods. The woods have ideal conditions for wild garlic to grow. The cows loved wild garlic and if they got into the woods in the springtime, you could smell their breathe as they came in for milking. Unfortunately, it was not only their breath that was affected and the milk would be tainted.

As you lifted the top of the churn off, you could smell it, once we did have churns of milk returned because of the taint. When having breakfast cereal, one taste of the milk was enough. It was like eating a sloe and my taste buds would dry up with the taste. We could not have cereals, so we had bacon and eggs for breakfast. What do you think the hens in the orchard were eating?

Yes! Garlic! YUUUUUK!

Even as I write this, I can remember the taste! You would think that some famous chef would find a recipe for such a delicacy.

The twenty cows all had names. After leaving school, I found some bits of wood, painted them white and wrote the cows name and ear tag number on them. I then hung them up above each stall. Frances, Susan, Gillian, Mandy, Davinia, Christine, Lindsey, Jill, Sabrina, Kelly, Jessie, Pixie, Buttercup, Ermindrude and Mildred. (Not bad Brin, after forty- five years.)

The hedges at Withan are still the same, although they are now trimmed with a flail trimmer, we still leave three feet of growth each side of the stone hedges to protect them. All the hedges have a string of barbed wire around them to keep the cattle from rubbing the hedge. This is easier in the long run than letting the cattle get through a hedge and making a gap that takes years to regrow and fill in. Some of the hedges are good stone- faced hedges and some are nothing more than a mound of soil. The brambles and hawthorn create a cattle proof barrier on the poorer hedges and the barbed wire make them even more impenetrable.

Many of the fields bordered the woods, with no hedge dividing them. Keeping the cattle out of the woods has been a never- ending task in my farming life. Always fencing, either a tree falling on the fence or bind weed growing around the fence and then dragging it down so the cattle could walk over it. If the cattle got into the woods, they could walk for miles and were very difficult to spot. Especially if they crossed the Creek and walked up to Kestle. I have spent many a happy hour, trudging through hundreds of acres of woods, looking for errant livestock.

The Seventies

During the 1970s, the dairy industry was changing, as milk churns were replaced by bulk collection. Instead of water cooling the milk, then the milk churns being left on the milk stand, to warm up in the sun, the milk in the bulk tanks was cooled by iced water to four degrees and agitated regularly and the temperature kept at four degrees. The keeping quality of the milk must have increased by a myriad amount at this period. We installed our first bulk tank in April 1977. A 250-gallon Fullwood tank that cost us £1900. We also installed a pipeline milking system at the same time. This did away with the bucket units.

Already, physical work was being eliminated. The milking units simply plugged into the pipeline and the milk flowed to a large sealed jar and was then pumped into the bulk tank, through a filter. A number of dairy farmers finished milking at this time, being unwilling to justify the expense of a bulk tank. At the time of installing the bulk tank, we were milking thirty cows and had the capacity to tie up thirty- four. During the next twelve months, we lengthened the lower cows house, from fourteen cow capacity to thirty and installed pipeline milking in the new standings. By the end of 1978, we were milking forty- eight cows and had space for fifty.

During the winter of 1974, the cows had all been inseminated to a Friesian bull, in anticipation of starting to expand the herd as we left school, but of the twenty cows, eighteen of them had bull calves. Very frustrating to a seventeen-year-old. To help increase numbers, Mother went to a sale at Falmouth and bought six pedigree bulling heifers, Killigrew Thetis, Tamara, Tiara, Tamsyn and two others! (Good grief Brin, can't you remember, it is only forty- five years ago.)

At the time of leaving school, we had one tractor at Withan. A Massey Ferguson 135 that was 47 horse power and we had bought new in 1973. This was when safety cabs had first become available on tractors and it was thought with Withan's hills and our history, it was a sensible move to have a cab on the tractor. We also had a scraper and transport box. The sum total of our machinery. The machinery that my father had accumulated, was sold at the farm sale when we left Trewothack. The car that Mother owned and Chris and I drove for the next five years, was an Austin Maxi (pretty street Cred!)

I passed my driving test in December 1975 and having joined Helston & St Keverne Young Farmers Club a couple of months earlier, we had more freedom, no longer having to be dropped off and picked up. With my cousins on the next farm, Philip and Roger and Chris, my brother, the Maxi started to travel a lot more miles to YFC events. When Grandpa asked how far we were going, I would say, "Just the other side of Redruth!" This could mean anywhere from Redruth to Launceston and St Teath to Lostwithiel.

In the month after leaving school, we planted the Slates Close in kale, soon after planting, there was a terrific storm with torrential rain, thunder and lightning. A lot of the soil from the Slates Close was washed through the gateway, along with the kale seed. We did have a marvellous crop of redshank, a weed also known as pig's bladder. This taught us that we needed to keep an eye on our crops and not to assume that everything would grow without problems.

By the summer of 1976, my uncles were preserving their grass as silage, although we still made all hay, we would be called upon to help with the silage. Our tractor would drive the grass mower. A Kidd Ultimow, this mower was a trailed machine with offset wheels and a six- foot cut. As the mower was lifted out of the grass at the end of the bout, it would lift one side at a time, looking like a drunken crab.

Our tractor had a safety cab covered with canvas and our little transistor radio would sit snugly between the cab and the canvas. An ear piece would then plug into the radio and the other end would fit into one side of our ear defenders. We could then hear the tinny sound from medium wave radio 1 in one ear. The only tractor with a radio at the time. To me, the best music was made in the late seventies!

If you leave me now by Chicago.
More than a feeling by Boston.
Mamma Mia, Fernando and Dancing Queen by Abba.
Don't go breaking my heart by Elton John and Kiki Dee.
Mississippi by Pussy Cat.
Young hearts run free by Candy Staton.
Woah, I'm going to Barbados by Typically Tropical.
Anything by The Eagles or Fleetwood Mac.
Beach Baby by First Class.

I could imagine a beach baby, in her bikini, riding around with me as I mowed the grass, admiring my tractor driving skills.

(…in…your…dreams…Brin…!)

Anyway!

While mowing, I would mow seven rounds around the field and then take a cut through the remaining grass, trying to keep the block of grass parallel, so there were no short ranks in the field. A skill that I was always trying to perfect.

We did not have set jobs while doing silage, so one day I could be mowing, the next forage harvesting, the next pulling trailers and the next buck raking the silage. The forage harvester was a New Holland double chop. It was pulled by a Massey Ferguson 185. All seventy-five horse power of her.

There were no electric or hydraulic controls on the double chop, just a handle through the back of the cab to adjust the spout and make sure the grass did not end up on the floor. There was no reverse drive either, so if there was a blockage caused by a lump of grass or momentary lapse in concentration, then the machine had to be stopped and cleared by hand.

A very tedious job, especially when the grass was jammed in solid and the spout chucked right up. A half an hour would go in no time. The trailers were pulled by a Ford 3,000 and a Zetor. The trailers were made out of old lorry butts and the tailgates had to be unlatched and latched manually. They held around four to five tonnes of grass and were driven into the yard and tipped up next to the silage pit, ready to be pushed away.

The silage was put away by another MF 135, (without a radio). It had dual wheels to give it added stability and a push off buckrake fixed on the back. The 135 was slightly under powered and small for the job, if pushing silage away all day, you knew you had done a day's work. I would be moving the tractor controls in my sleep. The art of the job was to reverse into the pile of grass and tease a useful amount onto the buckrake, then reverse is onto the pit and use the push off part to place a small layer over the grass that was already there, without leaving lumps.

If there were lumps, it was like mogul skiing and you could be thrown off the tractor seat while reversing and as you were looking backwards, it could also wrench your back. It was also imperative not to get stuck, because while you were being pulled out, the trailers of grass were still being tipped in the yard and it was difficult to get on top of the job again. While buckraking, the tractor spent half the time with its front wheels in the air because of the weight of the grass on the back. You learned to steer by the independent brakes.

On a good day in 1976, we could clear eleven acres of grass. It is hard to believe that in those years that I have been farming, we are now looking to clear at least eleven acres an HOUR and a hundred acres a day with a modern self-propelled harvester, albeit with six times the horse power. Most silage is now put away by a buckrake on the front of the tractor, making it a much kinder job on the tractor driver's back.

If the weather is kind and the machinery is behaving itself, I have always enjoyed making silage and I still do, although now with a 140 horse power Massey Ferguson and a twelve-tonne trailer. I do realise that at the age of sixty- two, my years of pulling silage are drawing to a close and I hope I have the wit to know when to call it a day and not have the decision forced upon me.

In July 1976, we doubled our tractor fleet to two. We needed a tractor with a front-end loader, to avoid having to borrow one and allowing ourselves to be more independent. The tractor we bought was another Massey Ferguson. A 35X, 45 hp, much older than our other tractor, but still useful. We paid £725 for it from Denis James of Porkellis. This tractor meant we could both go to work with a tractor when necessary. Chris was quite handy mechanically and made the loader into a power loader, by welding hydraulic rams on to tip the bucket or fork.

1976 was also the year of the great heatwave and the temperature got up to 95 degrees at the end of June. Every day was hot and dry. The grass disappeared and the well ran dry. For a time, the cows had to drink from the streams surrounding the farm and the pond half way up the lane. We also ran a pipe from the pond to the dairy to enable us to cool the milk in the churns. As the grass was so short, due to the drought, the cows were allowed up the lane, to graze the verges.

The lane was known as Long Meadow, I suppose grazing Long Meadow, sounded better than, grazing the lane. There was no water in the house either, which was not ideal, as mother had B&B visitors staying. Luckily, they looked on it as an adventure. We eventually cured the problem by running a pipe from the mains water at Mudgeon. This gave the well a respite and allowed it to supply the farm with water, for at least some of the time.

Many of the hedges in the parish caught fire, resulting in the fire brigade having to come and extinguish the flames. It was believed the fires were started by a local pyromaniac, but nothing was ever proved. The downs at Goonhilly also caught fire. This was on an evening when the Young Farmers Club had a beach evening at Poldhu. It felt like the flames were about to appear over the hill and surround the beach, such was the fury and heat of the fire.

The Slates Close was in barley and under-sown with grass seeds. When the barley was combined, there seemed no way that the grass seeds would survive. They were just dry wisps of grass. However, as soon as the rain did start in earnest, the seeds immediately greened up and grew, looking like they were trying to make up for lost time. Nature is a wonderful thing.

By the end of 1976, we were well involved with YFC and the year ended with the annual Carol Service and Dance. The service was always held in Truro Cathedral and the dance took place In Truro City Hall. Philip and I went. (Just the other side of Redruth!). Unfortunately, I left the Maxi's headlights turned on, as we parked before the service, by the time we returned to the car, after the dance, the battery was stone dead. All our friends had gone home and there were no mobile phones in those days. We tried to run the car off but there was not enough life in the battery for that. Eventually, we rang Uncle Ronnie from a phone box and asked him to pick us up.

We got home at quarter past four. Uncle Ronnie never said a word. After a couple of hours sleep, I got up and milked the cows, THEN Uncle Ronnie came and told me what he thought of me (and it was not much!) That day is etched on my memory, returning to Truro with a tractor battery and starting the car, travelling in my other uncle's Land Rover to Truro, sitting in the side seats, never a good idea when you are feeling a little under the weather. Then travelling home, wishing the day would end, so I could get into bed and catch up on my beauty sleep.

By the late seventies, I was entering speaking competitions in YFC, Brains Trust and Debating. I also discovered Tug of War, who would believe that pulling on a rope could be such fun. As I was left-handed, I pulled on the other side of the rope to the rest of the team. I was fortunate in representing Cornwall YFC at the National finals for several years, along with the rest of the team.

There was a Tug of War competition at YFC County Rally, if you won there, you represented the County at the South West finals, which were usually held at Royal Cornwall Show or Bath and West Show. The first two teams then went on to the National finals, that were held at The Royal Show, Stoneleigh, Warwickshire. The first year our YFC represented the County was in 1978, when we came fourth. The next year 1979, we came runners up (wait for the next exciting instalment!)

We were now making four and a half thousand small bales of hay annually, some good and some bad. But all hard work. As was the fertiliser, our order in 1979 was:

8 tonnes Nitro top.
6 Tonnes Extra Grass.
2 Tonnes Universal 15.
3 Tonnes 52 Regular.
6 Tonnes After Cut.

Twenty- five tonnes that all came in June and all twenty-five tonnes were in 1cwt (50 kilo) bags. All had to be unloaded by hand and stored and then handled again when being spread. These days our fertiliser comes in 600 kilo bags and all the work is done by the tractor loader.

1979 started with snow. The milk tanker could not get around, we pumped the milk into a thick plastic bag, specifically for that purpose and then pulled it down to St Erth in a trailer. This was done for a couple of days. The bag was difficult to wash out and I don't think it would have done many journeys, before leaking or starting to smell badly.

In November 1979, we dug the tarmac off the lane, in preparation for concreting it. The potholes were getting worse with the milk tanker coming in every day. I seem to remember wearing out a pick axe by digging that tarmac, or I may have imagined that I had that capacity for hard work! We laid twelve loads of concrete over three days. A real pain as it had to be laid going up-hill and that made the job even harder.

The cost was £120 per 6 cubic metre- load. I wish I could buy it for that now. The calves we sold at market that year averaged £70. One and a half calves to pay for a load of concrete. I have just checked the price of calves in the last week from a local auctioneer's. The average is £190. A 6-metre load of concrete is now £540. You do the maths! As an aside, in the seventies, if you sold calves at market, it was possible to be paid in cash on the same day. Difficult to believe nowadays, when cash seems to be a dirty word.

The Eighties

1980 started quite well, as at the YFC Carol service and dance in December 79, I had discovered the opposite sex and was courting (or sparking, as my grandpa's sister would say). This was a pleasant time for three months, until it ended in March. The day after we finished, I hedged up the Lambs Close gateway and still when I walk through that gateway, I remember that day! (Man-up Brin!)

We bought a mini pickup in the spring. Green and P reg, we paid £1075 for her. It was so useful for taking calves to market, going to farm sales and gave us a bit more freedom, if Chris and I needed to travel in different directions or had different destinations. The poor thing did not get much mercy.

That spring, our Tug of War team were training in earnest. Twice a week training and as many competitions as we could get to. Training consisted of pulling a weight up a tree by a series of pulleys, first individually and then as a group. It was hard work. Then to improve our fitness even farther, we started running after training, two to three miles each time.

To start, with I hated it, during the first part I would get a stitch, then I would throw that off and finish strongly. Later, I ran through the stitch and ran all the way and enjoyed the pain. After the sweat lost during pulling the weights, the run in the twilight was somehow refreshing. At the age of twenty-one, I was the fittest I had ever been. We needed to be fit for the YFC Nationals.

The South West finals were held at the end of May at The Bath and West Show. It was not a show that I enjoyed, as it had already started to lose its agricultural roots and it was difficult to find many tractors or farm implements. (What kind of show is that?) There were five teams there, Somerset, Wiltshire, Devon, Dorset and us, representing Cornwall. We came second, which qualified us for Nationals.

Nationals were held at The Royal Show, held at Stoneleigh, Warwickshire. It is hard now to explain, just what the Royal Show meant to the agricultural community. The show was held across four days in the first week of July and ran from 1839 to 2009. During the eighties, it would attract an attendance of 130,000. Many Agricultural Institutions had a permanent presence at Stoneleigh, among them Young Farmers Club, whose main office was based there. The NFU has its national office there. The Rare Breeds Trust. JCB. Many of the Breed Societies. The main Banks also had a permanent presence there. The National Dairy Unit and National Pig Unit were also based there.

There were four car parks surrounding the showground, with a large balloon flying over each entrance that could all be seen from some distance. These car parks were approached by different roads, so hopefully minimising travel congestion. Our usual entrance was car park four. We parked, then walked across the bridge over the river. This passed the acres of flood plain, that sported massive irrigators, that were sucking water out of the river and depositing it on the flood plain, demonstrating their potential to minimise the problems of another drought (1976).

The weather at Stoneleigh in July was usually very sultry, with a good chance of thunder storms. I attended the Show from 1977–83, usually pulling Tug of War, when the show was at its peak. The biggest stand on the Show was probably the Massey Ferguson stand, their factory was based in Coventry, not many miles from Stoneleigh, their stand exhibited every tractor they produced, from the humble MF 550 to the MF1200.

The MF1200 was a large pivot steer tractor with four equal size wheels and a mid- mounted cab, although it was a very impressive looking tractor and I quite fancied one at the time, it was only 105 horse power and would have been pretty useless on our hills. The Massey stand also had huge combines and balers on show. Most of them quite impractical for the far West of Cornwall and much more suited to the fields of the Cotswolds and East Anglia. (But who wants to look at tiny tractors?)

The machinery section was huge, with many now long-gone firms or under foreign ownership, showing off their cultivation equipment, ploughs, power harrows, mowers, forage harvesters, trailers. Anything you could think of. The JCB building had a patch of ground in front of their building that they used to demonstrate their diggers and loading shovels, must have been worth a fortune to them. Demonstrate the machinery and make a sale on the spot.

The woodland area formed a separate enclave of the show, the forestry commission were based there, along with trade stands, selling chain saws and strimmer, stands selling machinery for digging up and replanting trees and all manner of woodland related firms.

Land Rover also had a demonstration area and it was possible to ride around a specially built course in a Land Rover or a Range Rover. This course had several steep slopes and deep muddy ditches with huge potholes, demonstrating the off- road capacities of the vehicles. The tractor pulling course was nearby, with souped up tractors sporting massive twin chrome exhaust pipes, trying to pull a heavy sledge the length of the course. It did not matter if they did not succeed, as long as the engine was roaring and there was a vast column of smoke belching out of the exhaust pipes.

There were half a dozen large sheds at one part of the showground that housed the livestock, that were at the show to be judged. The cattle, many of them with famous prefixes from all over the country, there hoping to win the ultimate prize of The Royal Show Supreme Champion. This area had a judging ring nearby and the ring was surrounded by many of the breed society's stands and the semen companies. This ring was where the preliminary rounds of the Tug of War competition were held.

Our Tug of War kit consisted of black rugby shirts, black shorts white socks and working boots with heel irons fixed to them. Our Club's name was emblazoned on the back of the shirts:

Helston & St Keverne.

YFC.

Tug of War.

The day of the competition, we walked around the show in our kit, eyeing up the opposition, who were doing the same to us, trying to keep a lid on the adrenalin that was building up. The competition started in the early afternoon, there were two groups of six teams, with the winner of each group meeting in the final. There was a bit of gamesmanship going on, as there were two teams from Yorkshire, the strongest team, Yorkshire A, called themselves Yorkshire B in order to avoid what they perceived to be the strongest group. This actually did us a favour, we were all pretty wound up and pulled like men possessed, beating Yorkshire B and all the other teams in two straight pulls and getting to the final.

The final was held in the main ring of the show. The ring where famous show jumpers were riding, where the best cattle in the world were parading and where world class entertainment enthralled the crowds and then us.

Dartmouth YFC from Devon and Helston& St Keverne YFC from Cornwall. The two teams from the South West in the final for the second year in succession. The final was a three ender with us taking the first end, Dartmouth the second and with a terrific effort, we took the third end and became National Champions. One of my proudest moments as it took four years of practise and extreme hard work to achieve, but is something that can never be taken away. It was the first time that Cornwall had ever won and it would take Cornwall another thirty years before they won the competition again.

The spring of 1981 started wet and cold, we ran out of silage on 24 March and the cows were turned out into the grass. It was not an ideal situation and we were chasing around, buying hay from various places nearby. It let us know that we did not have all the answers, although at that age, you think you have most of them! As the fields were so wet, the cows were stepping them up and exacerbating the situation by ruining the grass.

The cow's milk was dropping daily because of lack of grass and our reluctance to graze the silage fields for fear of being in a worse position the next year. We were making silage as well as hay by this time, because of the wet weather, first cut silage started on the 22nd May and did not finish until 13th June. A very catchy year. We had increased our tractor fleet again and had bought a Leyland 272. This tractor was seventy- two horse power and had a quiet cab, so no need for ear defenders when driving it. It also had a fitted radio! Luxury indeed.

We planted flatpole cabbages in July, to feed the cows in the winter. uncle Ronnie thought it was a good idea. We thought it was designed to keep us busy, both in the summer when planting them and again in the winter, when we cut them and brought them in for the cows to eat.

We were now renting twenty- four acres at Roscruge from uncle Geoffrey, some three miles away, which gave us more scope. We were still milking by pipeline and this restricted cow numbers to a maximum of fifty. We started selling calved heifers at Helston Market and some of them made up to 600 guineas, which was pretty good money at the time, although we would rather have milked them ourselves. Some weeks we were topping the market for heifers and calves which were making up to £100. I tried not to look too smug; it is no good looking too happy until the hammer went down.

In the Young Farmer world, we arranged a twenty- four hour ploughing marathon. We were fortunate to borrow four tractors from local dealerships. Two of these tractors were brand new and were four-wheel drive. Four- wheel drive tractors were just becoming available and we quickly saw the greater potential those tractors had for grip and stability.

During the twenty- four hours, the four tractors ploughed a total of one hundred and thirty- five acres. I can still remember going to see one of the tractors and seeing the exhaust and manifold glowing red, as she ploughed on throughout the night. No mercy! We were fortunate to be able to raise £3,000 for the leukaemia unit at Treliske Hospital. I was privileged to be elected chairman of the club in the autumn.

Tremayne had come up for sale and as it bordered Mudgeon, we were hoping to buy it with Uncle Ronnie. We made an appointment with our bank manager, who, up till then, we had no dealings with. He was willing to lend us the money we needed, at the interest rate of 3% over base rate. We came out pleased that we could have the money. Tremayne was sold by formal tender, this meant all bidders putting their best offer in an envelope, sending it off and hoping for the best. Our bid was not accepted and another farmer bought it. (Since then, my cousin Philip, who farms Mudgeon has bought Tremayne.)

We were grazing the heifers at Roscruge and while driving up to see them, we would pass Lannarth Farm. Lannarth was for sale, but was too expensive for us to buy, however, the house and yard with two fields was sold, then the hills. Eventually there was thirty- five acres left for sale, Chris and I went in to have a look. The land was supposed to be wet and cold, but looked alright to us. Some of it was stony and it was north facing, but so was Withan.

We saw the owner, Mr Ankerson, and he told us how much he wanted for the thirty- five acres. We visited the bank manager again and being a bit wiser, managed to borrow the money for 2% over base rate. We paid £1080 an acre for the thirty-five acres. £36,000 in total, the same amount as my father and uncle had paid for Trewothack, some fifteen years previous. Talk about inflation.

Lannarth was signed over to us in February 1982, the next step was to pay for it! All the talk at the time was of calving heifers at two years old instead of three and we had decided to try two-year calving. This meant that instead of ten or a dozen in calf heifers, we had over twenty and with nowhere to milk them, we sold ten in calf heifers to one buyer for £565 apiece. This practically paid off our borrowed money, but realistically did us no favours, as we thought money could easily be paid back, which proved not to be the case in the future.

During that stage in my life, holidays did not really feature and travelling to The Royal Show to pull Tug of War for a couple of days was all the time off I needed. With help with £10 expenses from County and a free entry ticket to the Show, I was happy. However, that spring I decided to join the YFC bike hike from Truro to Blackpool, some four hundred miles, along with fifty other Cornish Young Farmers. I bought a ten-speed bike with dropped handlebars and did a bit of practising around the roads of west Cornwall.

We set off from Truro on 24th April 1982 and for the next seven days, cycled around seventy miles each day and stayed in Fire brigade training stations, council buildings, hockey clubs and the Malvern Showground, before cycling into Blackpool, being warned not to drop a bike wheel into the Blackpool tram tracks. We were welcomed by the Mayor of Blackpool and then found our hotel. That night we went to the YFC dance held at the Tower Ballroom, along with hundreds of other Young Farmers from all over the country.

A very impressive building. I believe I got to know more Young Farmers in that single week than in my previous six years of being involved with YFC.

I had known Ruth Thomas since she was three years old. She was a cousin of two of my primary school friends and was always at their birthday parties with her younger sister and her two older siblings. However, when chairing a YFC meeting, I looked up to see her big blue eyes looking at me and I had a bit of a heart flutter and thought I had better do something about it.

Something, was going to sports practise, then on to a disco at Smugglers, which turned out not to be on and then to a disco in a barn at Praze. After a couple of slow dances, we returned to our straw bale, somehow still holding hands! Ruth maintains that I did not let go of her hand, but I am sure she did not let go of mine. Anyway, we are still holding hands nearly forty years later.

Although we were making silage to feed the cows, silage and a tie up cow's house were not really compatible, as we could not feed the silage in the cow's house and had to let the cows loose to eat the silage and they were lying all over the yard by night. It was not an ideal situation, so we decided to bite the bullet, borrow some more money and build a shed that would house seventy cows in cubicles with a covered silage pit at the centre. That was 1983's project and it was intended to allow us to expand our dairy herd to seventy cows and not to restrict us to fifty as pipeline milking had done.

Unfortunately, milk quotas were introduced in early 1984. These were intended to stop over production of milk in Europe. A farms milk quota was decided by taking their 1982 production and taking away 9 %. For us it was disastrous! We had a provisional quota of 192,000 litres, but managed to get up to 212,000 litres by claiming hardship. 212,000 gave us enough milk quota to milk thirty- five cows. We had a shed to pay for that was budgeted for us milking seventy cows and we could milk half that number. Milk quotas properly screwed up our farming for years. We could not have timed things worse.

If quotas had been introduced a couple of years before, we would not have built the shed and carried on milking in the cow's house. If they had been introduced a couple of years later, we would have been milking seventy and been given a much bigger quota. Eventually, it became possible to rent and buy milk quota. Some farmers, nearing retirement, sold their cows and their quota. For them it was like having two herds to sell and made them a fortune.

Some younger farmers decided to cash their quota in and invest in some other enterprise. For us, that was not an option worth thinking about. We were dairy farmers. We had been dairy farmers for generations and we had been taught to hold on to the cow's tail and she would pull us through!

Some made fortunes, some lost them. Over the next twenty odd years, we spent a fortune on buying milk quota, trying to get big enough to make large profits. A futile exercise. I wonder if I went back to that time, with the benefit of hindsight, would I do anything different?

In order to help negate the impact of quotas, in 1984 we grew a field of broccoli in the Parc Bullock. Six acres, it kept us busy in the winter and spread our financial risk. The broccoli was marketed through GMS. We sent them off in large bins to the packhouse, where they were packed and graded for the supermarkets and anything not making the grade was sold to a firm making piccalilli. No waste!

Unfortunately, these days, anything that is not perfect is thrown away. At that time a broccoli head that a mouse had nibbled, could be scalped by a broccoli knife and still used for human consumption. Whether we will ever get back to that time is debatable, probably not until food becomes in short supply and we become grateful for bent carrots and scalped broccoli once more!

During 1984, Ruth and I got engaged after two years courting. We had been to the cinema and watched Jaws 3 and I suppose I was overwhelmed by the emotion of the occasion and proposed. Thankfully, Ruth said yes. I then had to ask her father for permission to marry his daughter!

He said, "Nobody could be happier about it than me, Brindley!" (Just thought I would slip that in.)

We were married in Sithney Church on 6th September 1985, followed by a reception at The Cottage Hotel, Carbis Bay. (Carbis Bay is where the next G7 is being held! Ahead of the game, or what!) We spent our weeks honeymoon in a caravan in North Wales. Nowadays, they seem to spend more and travel farther on their stag and hen parties than we did on our honeymoon. (Stop sounding so old, Brin.) We were fortunate that Withan farmhouse could be divided and we settled into half the house, with Mother and Chris living in the other half.

We increased our broccoli acreage and also grew some spring cabbage. I loved cutting broccoli. With the right oilers on and my back to the weather, it could rain, hail or sleet, it made no difference. With a twelve- inch broccoli knife, I would cut and trim the heads. Searching out the heads ready for cutting and nicking off the rubbish with a swipe of the knife. A hazardous pursuit, but I only cut myself once in many years of cutting broccoli.

I took a swipe with the knife and caught my knee. It meant a visit to the Doctor for a couple of stitches and a stiff knee for a week. Cutting cabbage, by contrast, I hated. They all had to be cut and it was a matter of head down, ass up, and then pack forty pounds of cabbage into a crate. The cabbage crop was an insurance. If a hard snow or frost came in and killed the broccoli, the price of cabbage would increase and hopefully make up for the loss of the broccoli. Cabbage played hell with my back and the only time I enjoyed cutting them was when they were selling for £10 a box (I only remember that happening once).

Boden came up for sale in 1987. It bordered Lannarth and so we pushed the boat out even farther and agreed to buy forty acres. The price of land had doubled in the six years since we had bought Lannarth and so we paid £2,000 an acre (you do the maths). We also bought 70,000 litres of milk quota that brought our total quota up to 300,000. We were having to spend thousands of pounds to try and get to a position of having a dairy herd large enough to be sustainable. Particularly galling, when many of our neighbours received a sustainable quota without spending a penny (23 pence a litre for that milk quota comes to mind!)

As I was coming up to my thirtieth birthday, Ruth was pregnant, but unfortunately, had a miscarriage. She was taken to Barncoose Hospital, along with the many girls who were there for an abortion. The Doctors may have been well qualified to treat the physical symptoms, but the treatment of the emotional turmoil was a Disgrace.

Later, I wrote a letter of complaint to the hospital of Ruth's treatment, whether it did any good I do not know. I can only hope that these days, Doctors are trained in compassion and not just surgery. I spent my thirtieth birthday collecting Ruth from hospital and bringing her home. A hard time for both of us.

By the end of the decade, we were milking fifty cows, the same number as we started the decade with. Progress! On the plus side, we had bought seventy- five acres of land and were still in business. I had also met Ruth, got married and on the 30th December1989 our first daughter Sarah was born. An ideal end to the decade!

My grandfather and his siblings milking cows at Clowance Barton Farm during the 1930`s

My great grandfather walking up Coinagehall Street, Helston on a market day durig the 1940`s

My grandpa Hosken and his dog

My uncle, father, auntie, great grandfather and grandfather standing in front of a newly built rick during the 1950`s

My father, brother and I at Chywoone Farm 1963.

Meeting Princess Anne at the Young Farmers County Rally aged fourteen 1974

Becoming Young Farmers Tug of War national champions 1980

Posing before pulling Tug of War 1983.

Cutting winter cauliflower 1990's

The pedal tractor that is now being used by the next generation 1995.

Garden Party at Buckingham Palace 2018

Travelling back from one of our coast path walks during Covid 2020.

Finishing the 630 miles of the South West Coast Path 2021.

Standing on Withan Quay, Frenchman`s Creek 2022

Ready to start silage at Treveador, overlooking the Helford River.

Driving the tractor down one of Cornwall`s many narrow lanes.

Brindley, his three children and Patch.

The Nineties

We started the nineties by coming to terms with being parents. Sarah was a very placid baby and was sleeping through the night by the time she was six weeks old. We were very smug and complacent and decided it was all to do with routine. We had all the answers. We were so clever, until the spring, when Ruth started being sick in the mornings! The doctor confirmed that she was pregnant again (not so clever now, eh, Brin!). For a time, we thought we might have had two in twelve months, but we managed to stretch it out to a fortnight over.

On the farming front, we were milking about fifty cows, rearing all the calves for replacements or beef, growing broccoli and cabbage and growing barley to feed to the cattle. Milk quotas were still causing us big problems and during January 1991, we were feeding nearly fifty gallons of milk a day to the calves, in an attempt to get rid of the milk that we did not have enough quota for. Our aim was for our annual production to be 5% over our 300,000-litre quota.

There was only a fine if the country as a whole exceeded its annual quota and 5% over was a risk worth taking. The fine was more than the price that the milk would bring and the risk of that could not be ignored. We bought a second-hand bulk milk tank from a dairy farmer who had seen the light and cashed his cows and quota in. (Not our way! We were dairy farmers!) This tank held 540 gallons and was referred to by Ruth's father as, "The Queen Mary!" We paid £900 for it and sold our old 250- gallon tank for £500. The Queen Mary was bigger than we needed at the time, but it was not stupid money.

David was born in January 1991, at least we had a calendar year between them! David was not a content baby. He was two years old before he slept through the night and knocked our smugness about, "routine" into a cocked hat.

During February, we had snow and an east wind, with temperatures down to minus 7. The broccoli was selling well and we received £7.70 home for boxes of twelve. Unfortunately, some of the broccoli we cut later in the month had suffered frost damage. We did not realise that when cutting them, but they started smelling when they got to market. (Frosted broccoli smell absolutely abominable, a bit like rotting flesh. I can smell a field of broccoli that has been frosted from at least half a mile and it still turns my stomach).

After jumping through a lot of hoops and canvassing a load of County Councillors, we managed to get planning permission to build a bungalow at Lannarth. We had started trying shortly after buying Boden, so it took around four years. The bungalow was built during 91 to 92. It was timber framed with stone facing and was nearly finished in time for Chris and Caroline's wedding in May 1992.

During the next two years, we built a couple of sheds up Lannarth, in preparation for splitting our partnership. Chris and I had different outlooks and priorities and were clashing personalities. Most of my cousins and friends had been farming in their own right since they were in their mid-twenties. I was by now in my mid-thirties and reaching the age my father was when he died. I was depressed by my perceived lack of progress in my farming. My depression was not helped by my unwillingness to talk about my feelings and the mantra of, "A problem shared is a problem doubled!"

Meaning if I talked about it, there would be two of us worrying about it, instead of just me. I have friends who work with their brothers in seeming harmony, but we could not. We get on very well now we are no longer in business together. We split our partnership in 1996, with me continuing with the dairy herd at Withan and Chris continuing with the beef and broccoli at Lannarth.

Our family was completed in May 1994, when our younger daughter, Frances was born. Frances, like David, decided to wait until she was two years old before she slept through the night.

In late 1994, the Milk Marketing Board was abolished. The MMB had been introduced in 1933 to stop the milk buyers from abusing their market power. My grandfather told us that when the MMB came into fruition, his milk price doubled. Sixty years later, when it was abolished, the problems of milk marketing were still the same.

Namely, a product that could not be stored for more than a couple of days and a product that could not be switched on and off at the drop of a hat. As dairy farmers, we had the choice of signing up direct with a processor or signing up with a new cooperative, Milk Marque. We signed with Milk Marque, being cooperatively minded and considering we lived too far out in the sticks, to risk a processor considering us unviable and stopping collecting our milk.

At the time of the MMB's demise, our annual average milk price was about 21 pence per litre. This increased until 1996, when our average milk price reached 24 pence per litre. The way the milk was marketed was ripe for manipulation. The milk was offered for sale at a certain price and if it was oversubscribed, it was offered again at a higher price until the supply and demand matched. During 1997, when the milk was offered for sale, the large processors did not bid for two price rounds and so the milk price dropped substantially. The fact that none of the processors bid for the milk was just a coincidence and not pre planned. (Yeah! Right!) By the end of the decade our annual milk price had dropped to 17 pence a litre.

The price dropped even farther in the early 2000s. The irony was that Milk Marque was declared a monopoly and had to be split into three companies to stop them abusing their considerable power in manipulating the milk price!

In 1995, we started growing maize to feed the cows during the winter. It was a more reliable and stable crop than grass silage and would grow well during a dry summer. The perceived wisdom was that two forages would increase the cow's intake of food resulting in more milk. Maize is a lovely crop to grow, once it gets going, you can almost see it growing and that is very satisfying.

It is also a very healthy looking dark green. Knee high by the fourth of July is the aim. We grew maize in the Roadway Field one year. This field is surrounded by woods, so is very sheltered and it is also the field that gets the most farm yard manure, both from the cows and the spreader. Around the gateway, it grew to twelve feet tall. There is a video that my father- in- law filmed at the time, describing it has a master crop. I am just standing there looking smug.

During the 1990s, we had several cows who succumbed to BSE (mad cow disease). They would become very agitated about entering the parlour and would stand in the yard shaking on unsteady feet. Some of them would get quite violent, shaking their heads and snorting at me. I believe we had eleven taken over the years, with five of them being declared positive. All the five were from the same bull, Quarn Galore Craig.

In humans, the disease is known as Cruez-Jacob Disease or CJD. During March 1996, a new strain was found that was believed to have come from cow beef. Within twenty- four hours, twenty- six countries had banned British beef. Within a week, there was a worldwide ban on British beef and all associated products, ranging from vitamin pills to lipstick. It was later considered that the problem was only a risk from older cattle and a ban on cattle over thirty months entering the food chain was put in place. Cattle passports were introduced.

These gave the date of birth of the animal, its ear tag number, its mother's ear tag number and its breed. The calf had to be ear tagged within three days of birth and passports had to be applied for before the animal was twenty- seven days old. Cattle passports are still mandatory twenty- five years later, a bovine animal without one cannot be sold or enter the food chain and must be destroyed. This new system was very difficult for some farmers who struggled with paperwork and new regulations. It was no longer satisfactory just being a good stockman, you needed to be an administrator as well.

In this part of Cornwall, it is extremely difficult to get hold of more land. I have a friend who was offered to rent another 350 acres farther up the County, but on the Lizard, you are lucky to get hold of twenty acres. As our farm is bordered by the river, the problem is exacerbated. At the end of our lane, if you turn right, the land is reasonably level and land is at a premium, with many local farmers chasing every acre on offer. If you turn left at the top of our lane, the road slopes steeply to the stream at the bottom.

The stream marks the boundary between the Parishes of St Martin and Manaccan. The road is so steep, that on maps it has arrows on it. So steep, that we once had a trailer load of silage pull a tractor backwards while trying to get up it. The trailer climbed a bank and flopped over onto its side. It was a morning's work to sort it out.

That is the sort of hill it is. During the late 1990s, I managed to rent three blocks of land on the other side of the hill, in Manaccan Parish. Obviously farming them would have been easier without the hill but the land was as near as I was going to get.

The first block was part of Landrivick, four fields totalling twelve acres, six acres being hills. These were just across the valley from Withan and it was easy to drive the heifers along the road to them. The next block was part of Tregithew, three level fields, totalling sixteen acres and twelve acres of hills. (I hope you can see a pattern here! Hills!) The hills were the other side of the valley from Withan 's hills, but there was no path through, with woods and a fifty- yard stretch of boggy ground and a stream separating them.

Finally, the third block was part of Kestle. Twenty acres of level ground in two fields, a five- acre field and a fifteen-acre field. The owner, Boden Lyne, had passed retirement age and had sold his bullocks and rented the land to me. Although Boden was happy for me to reseed the small field, he would never let me plough the larger field. He would tell me that the field had not been ploughed for the whole of the twentieth century.

To me, that was all the more reason to plough it. The grass was not good quality with a load of hardheads growing in it. With hindsight, I should have cut it bare and overseeded it with grass and clover seed.

I farmed these three patches of ground for several years, before losing all three. At Landrivick, the owner's grandson left school and he took them back in hand. At Tregithew, the owner signed the land into a stewardship agreement. There was open access over all the land, there was to be no fertiliser spread, neither artificial or farm yard manure. There was to be no supplementary feeding of the grazing animals and silage could not be cut till the middle of July. And I had to subscribe to best agricultural practise.

I considered that if I was not allowed to feed the soil in any way, then I could not subscribe to best agricultural practise. Leaving silage making till July was also impractical, so I gave the land up. With hindsight, I should have kept it and worked around the rules, although inconvenient, I was never going to get hold of any land nearer to Withan. At Kestle, Boden Lyne sold the place. The new owners converted the decrepit barns and started an art gallery there.

I rented the land for a couple more years, but knocking down a gatepost to get the forage harvester through and then widening it by four feet, did not endear me to the owners (I did hedge it back up and put in a granite latching post!)

Unfortunately, the new owners decided they wanted the land farmed organically, so I lost that land as well. Pretty careless to lose all three blocks!

For several years after Chris and I split our partnership, I did all the milking fourteen milking's a week for fifty- one weeks of the year. Even when we went to the Royal Cornwall Show, I would milk before we went and again when we got back. It was pretty hard going as I was working a minimum of seventy hours a week and during harvesting considerably more, but I was building for the future. In the late nineties, Arther Noye came to work for us a couple of days a week. He did three milking's a week, which cut the grind of me doing every milking and eased the pressure of work.

We did always manage a week's holiday every year. It was important to me to take Ruth and the children off and give them my full attention for the week. We never travelled far as the children did not travel well and if one was sick, the other two would come out in sympathy. Usually, Devon or Somerset. South Hams, Dartmoor or Exmoor, getting up as far as Hereford on one occasion. I was always looking for a window of opportunity for a holiday, silage finished, corn cut, no cows calving. Opportunity! I was a right sod to Ruth, as she liked time to get prepared and sometimes, I would only give her forty- eight hours' notice. Silage covered down.

"Right! are you all right to go on holiday."

"When?"

"Saturday!"

Although my mother took us on holiday every year when we were children, we only went on holiday with my father once, when we stayed in a caravan near Bournmouth. I still treasure that week, as we visited London on the train and I got to spend some individual quality time with my father. Mother and Father would go off for a few days to Cambridge machinery sales sometimes. Father would go to the sale and buy stuff he thought he could make a profit on and mother would look around Cambridge. Apparently, my father did not give my mother much notice either!

By the end of the decade, we had bought more milk quota and our total quota was up to 350,000 litres. We were also leasing another 100,000 litres, which was costing us in the region of eight pence per litre. By then we were milking eighty cows and I was still keen on pushing forward, having just passed the age of forty. In that decade, we had built a bungalow, put up sheds, bought milk quota and split our partnership. On the negative side, we were relying heavily on borrowed money to fund the business.

The Noughties

The first of January 2000, the day when all computers were supposed to crash, all planes were supposed to fall out of the sky and complete mayhem was expected. That day came in like a damp squid, completely uneventful, with none of the disasters the doom mongers were predicting. But in February 2001, foot and mouth disease was discovered in a abattoir in Essex. By the time it was discovered, the disease had already spread to fifty- seven farms. The worst affected area was Cumbria, followed by Devon. There were several cases in Cornwall, all in the north of the County.

We placed old carpets soaked in disinfectant at the end of the lane and stopped all unnecessary visitors from coming to the farm. All the footpaths in the country were closed and even the general election was postponed. The Royal Cornwall Show was postponed from June until September. The disease was supposed to have originated from a farm in Cumbria that fed pig's swill. The outbreak resulting in the compulsory culling of six million animals, with 2,000 farms affected and many families traumatised, as their life's work and their reason for existence were shot, burned and buried.

The saying was:
Pigs catch it!

Sheep spread it!

Cattle show it!

Twenty years ago, a lifetime to some and a blink of an eye to others. I must confess, I have not given Foot and Mouth any thought for years and only as I started writing did the memories come back. I wonder about the farmers who were directly involved, the ones who had their animals slaughtered, do they still have flash backs or has time dimmed the awful memories of that time in farming history?

By 2002, I was aware that renting land away from Withan was adding to our costs in a substantial way, but there was no chance of renting land that was touching Withan. I always had ambitions of farming Trewothack, or failing that, a farm that would match up to Trewothack. Something Withan was never going to do. I saw Castlezens advertised in a local paper and something drew me to it and I sent off for details.

Castlezens was on the Roseland peninsula, about two miles from Tregony and within a couple of miles from the south coast of Cornwall. The north coast of Cornwall has never drawn me, being harsher, with fewer tree lined coves and valleys. The Roseland was softer, more like the Helford area in character and appealed to me immediately.

Ruth and I decided to go and have a look around! Castlezens was 211 acres, all the land was touching, with a network of minor roads and lanes leading to all of the fields. There was only one field that did not border a road or lane. There was one block of land that consisted of forty acres in three fields. These three fields were nineteen, eleven and ten acres, gently sloping. Absolutely ideal for silage or maize. If they were touching Withan and I could have bought them, I would have died a happy man!

The farm house had been modernised and was in good order and ivy covered. The farm buildings were mainly traditional barns, with a couple of modern sheds. There was a valley between the blocks of land and another building across the valley. An ideal scenario, a farm ripe for a modern dairy set up, with just enough buildings to manage with in the short term.

The next week, Tony Harris from Lodge and Thomas came out and looked around Withan. I have to say, it was in good order, with all the gates hanging and a concrete water trough in each field. Although Withan was a pig to farm, it did have two big plusses. A chocolate box farmhouse AND it ran down to Frenchman's Creek, a local beauty spot, made famous by Daphne du Maurier's book of the same name. These two things made Withan more valuable than its worth as a working farm.

We decided to give it a go, but before we put Withan on the market, we had to tell the children. This did not go well and there were a lot of tears, not only from the children. We took them to Castlezens to look around and also took them to Portholland beach, which was only two miles away. They were still not convinced. I wrote in my first book, "Cows and Catastrophes", about their reaction, but I think it is worth repeating because it pretty much sums up their characters.

Frances was seven, "I am not going, unless I can have a pony!"

David was ten and thought that was an angle worth pursuing, "I am not going, unless I can have a quad bike!"

Sarah was eleven and soon to start comprehensive school, "I am not going, unless I can have a new pair of flares to wear to school!"

Withan was put up for sale and that stirred up the neighbourhood for a while. The whole summer seemed to be filled with showing prospective purchasers around Withan, some of them serious, some living in cloud cuckoo land and some obviously out for a jolly day out. There were some seriously considering buying and we were negotiating with Mr Berridge, the owner of Castlezens at the same time. He was a difficult man to pin down, we would make an offer, he would accept the offer and then say he wanted to keep three fields back.

Very difficult. We thought everything may have come together for a time, but in the end, we did not buy Castlezens and it was eventually sold to three different buyers. A pity such a farm was broken up, but nothing we could have done about it. We did also look around Leyonne Farm, near Fowey, we had driven through Par to reach the farm and that was not a pretty route. Leyonne had a lovely milking parlour and dairy set up, but the farm house would have needed a lot of money spent on it and it was farther up the County than we really wanted to move.

The two farms were complete contrasts, although they were both around two hundred acres. At Castlezens, the money had been spent on the farm house and very little on farm buildings. At Leyonne, the money had been spent on the farm buildings and very little on the farmhouse. In both cases, the owners had been able to amass two hundred acres of land in a ring fence.

That summer was very stressful, as we showed prospective purchasers around Withan, tried to negotiate with Mr Berridge and tried to work out a strategy for farming Castlezens in the short term. I also bought my first mobile phone at the time, having laughed at people using them at agricultural shows for years! At the time, it was very useful for Tony Harris to reach me at any time, concerning different people wanting to view Withan.

In the autumn, we took Withan off the market and I sat down and cried with frustration!

I declined to mention several chapters back that we installed a milking parlour during 1985. This parlour was a 8/8 low line parlour. This meant there were four cow standings each side with milk jars tucked underneath where the cows were being milked. This parlour was becoming quite decrepit. We were milking ninety cows through it and milking was taking three hours morning and evening and as I was still doing the majority of the milking, it was becoming soul destroying. We had put off doing anything while Withan was on the market, but in the spring of 2003, we started installing a new milking parlour.

The new parlour was being installed in the same building as the old parlour, so we had to find a way to milk the cows until the new parlour was up and running. We hired a parlour, which was a trailer with a gap in the middle for the milker to stand, with ramps front and back for the cows to enter and leave. A tarpaulin cover and a milk line running through the entire length.

We ran the cows through a couple of times, just to get them used to it and then with snow falling and the easterly wind blowing, we milked! The cows took to it like a duck to water and within three days, we had knocked an hour off each milking. Bliss! I could get out of bed half an hour later and still be in for breakfast a half an hour earlier. We milked in the bail for three months until the new parlour was ready to go.

The new parlour was a 12/24 direct to line with auto ID. This meant it held twelve cows each side and twelve milking units that moved from one side to the other. The milk went straight into the pipeline through an electrical meter that measured the amount of milk given by each cow. The auto ID recognised each cow as she entered the parlour and dropped the appropriate amount of cow cake into each trough. We also installed slot drainage.

These were inch slots running the length of the parlour, so when the cow's soiled the parlour, the offending solids could be washed straight away and not chased from one end of the parlour to the other. (Very restrained there Brin, I thought you were going to say Shit!)

I have to say, it was a lovely parlour to milk in and had been designed that anyone over six feet (me and David!) could milk in it without banging our heads. Nothing worse than having to keep ducking while milking.

At the time, we were feeding the grass silage behind a feed barrier placed there by the tractor loader. The maize was eight feet high and was eaten straight from the clamp, with an electric fence stopping the cows from eating too much. I walked into the shed one day just in time to see a two feet block of maize silage, running the width of the shed, break away and collapse, burying twenty cows, who were knocked to their knees. I nearly fell to my knees, I thought they were all dead! I grabbed the fork and ran to uncover them, but after thirty seconds, they all backed out and got back on their feet, leaving me trembling uncontrollably. The cows got over it before I did.

The new milking parlour made life easier as I was spending two hours a day less milking, so when we were offered the chance to go to Canada on a farming trip, we decided to take it. As it was a study trip, we also had some funding that helped make up our mind. Neither Ruth or I had been abroad or flown before, so everything was an experience. There were ten of us on the trip, four farming couples and two Semex reps.

Semex were running the trip. We took the bus from Plymouth to Heathrow and not being very savvy, I had not drunk anything on the bus and by the time we reached Heathrow, I was quite dehydrated and not feeling up to a six-hour flight. Luckily, I was told to drink water and I gradually felt better.

Heathrow was a revelation, it was like a town, with so many people milling around. There were people selling raffle tickets with a chance of winning an Aston Martin, (like James Bond!), which was parked in the thoroughfare. Cornwall could not have been described as cosmopolitan at the time, but Heathrow certainly was. I had seen orthodox Jews on television, but had not expected that they would travel abroad in their traditional hats and gowns. All part of life's rich tapestry!

I was very thankful that we had someone in charge, telling us where to go and what to do. Everything was totally alien to us. The plane we travelled on was a British Airways Boeing 777 and as we boarded, it was lovely to see how the first-class passengers were travelling, before we headed to the back of the plane and squeezed into our seats. We took off and then could hear the hydraulics working as the plane banked to change course.

I thought, "I would be happier if we were a bit higher before you do that, mate!" Ruth settled down to watch a film on the small screen in front of her, while I spent the entire journey watching the details of our flight, how high we were, how fast we were going, where we were and how cold the temperature was outside! Fascinating!

We landed at Montreal and as we had come from farms, questioned about whether we had mucky boots in our luggage. The Canadians were still worried about the Foot and Mouth outbreak that Great Briton had suffered three years earlier. We then met our driver, Bob Schmitt, and headed to St Hyacinthe where we were staying for the first couple of nights. St Hyacinthe was in the Quebec Territory; the surprise was the number of the population who spoke French and did not speak English (surely everyone should speak English!).

We spent the next couple of days visiting herds of cows with famous prefixes, Deslacs, Karona and Comestar. We were using bull semen from Comestar at the time, so that made the visit memorable. Although we were in the Quebec province, we did not get as far as Quebec City. I remembered Quebec from History in school, when General Wolfe and his men climbed the cliffs to Quebec, surprised the French and took the city for the British. History is more interesting if you have been to the places described in the history books.

Our next stay was in Ottowa, the Canadian capital city, where we spent the morning looking at the Canadian Houses of Parliament, based loosely on our own Palace of Westminster. It even had a clock tower. It felt odd that there was a bronze statue of the Queen on horseback in the City and yet the majority of the population spoke French. I suppose you have to live there to know how it all works in practise.

In the afternoon, we travelled to Gananoque. One hundred miles of driving through level scrub land, with the odd tower silo showing on the horizon and I thought Goonhilly Downs was barren! After we had settled into our hotel, Bob asked us if we fancied going to an ice hockey match that evening?

"Ummm, let me think! YES!"

The match was so fast and furious and as one player was smashed into the barrier, I distinctly remember doing a fist pump and shouting, "Geddon, my son! Wooooh!"

Felt quite ashamed of myself, but ice hockey is that kind of sport.

During the interval, a group of five-year olds came onto the rink, where they raced each other around the ice, chasing the puck like little penguins.

It was a brilliant night and we will always treasure it.

Many of the farms we visited on that trip were specialist pedigree farms, with a large chunk of their income coming from selling bulls to semen companies. The other farms were normal commercial dairy farms. Almost all the farms were of the same basic design, a barn where the cows were tied up, with a tower silo holding silage attached, enabling the farmer to tend and feed the cows during the freezing winter months, without having to venture outside. Most of the herds were around sixty cows with two generations of farmers managing them. I reckon we visited around twenty- five farms in total.

There is a Mennonite area near Kitchener where the Amish farmed. We were fortunate that Bob lived in Kitchener and knew the area well and was willing to drive us through the area. It was an eye opener, as the fields were being ploughed and dung was being spread by horse and the local school had a hitching rail for horses, rather than a car park. It was an interesting experience, but it would have been good to have had the time to delve deeper into the why's and wherefore's of the Amish community.

After a week of farm visits, we headed into the centre of Toronto, to the five-star Intercontinental Hotel! (Just thought I would slip that in! It was the first and up till now, the last, five-star hotel we have stayed in)

Toronto was quite a contrast to west Cornwall! Once we had come to terms with the huge skyscrapers and city blocks, we discovered there was another City underground. During the winter, the climate is so cold and snowy that shopping underground becomes the normal. While we were in Toronto, we took the opportunity to travel to the top of the CN tower.

At a height of nearly 500 yards, the sky-pod had fantastic views over Toronto and Lake Ontario. The floor panel made of glass was a little off putting. I could walk on the edge of it by closing my eyes, but my body would not let me walk on it with my eyes open, however much reason told me that the glass had not broken in thirty years and was unlikely to break at the very instant that I walked on it.

Obviously, we were not in Toronto to visit dairy herds, but to visit the Canadian Royal Agricultural Winter Fair. Rather like our own Royal Show, but held in the winter instead of the summer, held inside instead of outside, still relevant to Canadian Farmers, still being held and still attracting 300,000 people to visit from all over Canada.

We spent two days at the show, looking at the show cows being judged, the horse rings, with the blue and yellow ribbons lining the roof, making the competitions even more of a spectacle. The corn sheaves, immaculately ribboned, ready for judging, reindeers, pumpkins, every sphere of Agriculture there, ready to be judged.

I would love to go back one day!

Our final day, we spent at Niagara Falls. My words cannot do it justice! Obviously, one of the wonders of the natural world and I count myself fortunate to have been there. We had dinner in a restaurant over-looking the falls and as the waitress threw my credit card back at me, I realised that tipping was not discretionary in that part of Canada. We left Niagara in the late afternoon, as the air turned cold and the spray from the falls made the air damp and feel colder still. (Cornish Cold!)

As we took off from Toronto airport, the noticeable sight, was the uniformity of the lights, lining the roads and forming perfectly square blocks, with not a kink in sight in any of them. Some hours later, as we approached Heathrow, the plane had to complete a circuit around East Grinstead to avoid arriving early and gave us a view of the jigsaw shapes, that were the hundreds of misshapen fields, miles beneath us.

Our Milk Cooperative, Milk Marque, had been scrapped by now, having been judged a monopoly. It was not deemed possible to split it into two cooperatives as that would have been a duopoly! A name I had not heard of before and not heard since. Milk Marque was divided into three and we signed up with Milk Link.

After a time, Milk Link wanted to change to every other day collection of milk and gain from the savings that would be gained by efficiency. There were financial incentives for going to every other day collection, so we bit another bullet and bought another bulk tank. If the old tank was The Queen

Mary, the new one was The Torrey Canyon, 1300 gallons or 6,000 litres capacity.

During the whole of that decade, the price we were getting for our milk was diabolical. By 2006, our annual milk price was less than sixteen pence per litre. This was two thirds of the price we received a decade earlier!

t is only when looking back years later, that you realise the future problems that were being planted by the unrealistic prices. At the time, you try and ride the storm, in the hope of better times ahead.

During 2007, we had a tuberculosis reactor, found during a routine test. Before then, the annual T.B. test at Withan was just an inconvenience and nothing to worry about. After finding a reactor, the future T.B tests meant a stressful week, with no guarantees of a clear test. After finding a reactor, we had to be retested every sixty days until we had two clear tests and the farm was shut down in that time, with no calves allowed to be sold. Financially difficult. I will nail my colours to the mast here and say I do believe in thinning out the number of badgers, where there is a T.B problem.

Spring 2008, I was offered the chance of going to Switzerland on a four- day farming trip. Yes please! We stayed in Charmey, near Bulle. The milk from the farms we visited was all used to make Gruyere cheese and because Gruyere cheese is not pasteurised, the cows were not allowed to eat silage because of the threat of listeria. They were all fed on barn dried hay. The farms supplying the Gruyere factory all transported their milk to the factory and some farms were still transporting their milk in ten- gallon milk churns.

We visited one farm where they had built a new farmhouse and cow shed in one building. Very impressive, but not for me. Many of the herds were milked in tie barns, as in Canada. We were in Switzerland in early April and you could see the snow line rising farther up the mountains each day. Such a beautiful country, I would love to go back and visit the mountain grazing dairy herds and find out their particular challenges. I did try Gruyere Fondue but again, not for me.

The milk price had risen by the middle of 2008, but the price of tractor diesel had doubled in twelve months, from 34 pence per litre to 68 pence, making our off ground even more expensive. Fertiliser prices had also doubled, farther reducing our margins. David was home working with me by now and Sarah was training to be a Veterinary nurse, which later became her career. By the end of 2008, we were milking 110 cows, each cow yielding 8,200 litres. The milk price had risen during 2008, nearly back to the price it was twelve years before.

I had reached the age of fifty in 2008 and was struggling to come to terms with it. Forty had not been a problem, but fifty really hit me. I was getting old and not really ready for it. The decade finished with the milk price dropping once more, creating more misery and stress and wondering what our next step to maintain our income could be.

The Tens A

The fundamental truths of business and personal finance;

Turnover is vanity!

Profit is sanity!

Cash is reality!

You cannot expand your way out of trouble!

Micawbers principle;

Annual income £20, annual expenditure £19. 50, result happiness!

Annual income £20, annual expenditure £20. 50, result misery!

I believe I have farming neighbours where cash is a reality. (I may be wrong!) You can tell by their clear eyes, with no hint of dark rings beneath them and their steady hands with no hint of a tremble. Unfortunately, cash had never been a reality for us, for many years we had tried to expand our way out of trouble and with every milk price cut, tried to increase our turnover to cover the loss of income.

We were not the only ones; most dairy farmers were doing the same. The supermarkets would squeeze the processors on price, the processors just passed the price cut to the producers, who milked another ten, twenty, hundred cows to make up the difference. We were like lemmings jumping off a cliff, because we could not see any other option. Always believing that soon things would come right, that the supermarkets would realise that all businesses needed to make a profit and start paying a realistic price, for a product that the vast majority of the population used every day.

How long do you go on thinking that?

I had been thinking it since the demise of the Milk Marketing Board, fifteen years previously. I knew we had specific problems, the hills at Withan, the off land and the extra costs involved with that land. The carrying forth of the expenditure of buying the land, that my brother farmed. The disastrous timing of milk quotas on our business.

The inability to get land touching Withan, where we could just push a gateway through a hedge to reach it. The Helford River bordering our farm, farther restricting our options to expand locally. We were technically sound, organised, on top of the work, but it still was not enough.

Things came to a head in September 2010. Ruth and I celebrated out Silver Wedding Anniversary, we had hoped to go on a cruise, but!

I had a meeting with my bank manager and consultant and was told we needed to get rid of our workman to save money. The next day, I went for a long walk and tried to find a way forward. I was fifty- two years old, I had worked extremely long hours for many years and although on top of the work physically, the financial mental strain was wearing me down and as I looked forward into the future, for the first time, I did not believe that anything would change for the better in the foreseeable future.

I did not have enough mental stamina to carry on as we had been and did not believe I had enough years left in my working life for things to come right.

Ruth asked me if I had found any answers. I replied that I did not think there were any and broke down and cried for the first time in eight years.

Cried in absolute frustration!

Cried that my father had died!

Cried that Withan was such a bitch to farm!

Cried that we had not managed to move farms!

Cried that I was not able to progress as I would have wished!

Cried that my best was not good enough!

Just cried!

I cried again three days later, as I told David that the cows had to be sold.

I had always hoped we could have got into a position where he would have been able to compete on a par with farming neighbours and not been hindered by the past, as we had been for all of our farming lives. But it was not to be!

Once the decision to sell the cows was made, I wanted to get on with it. I asked our vet, David Crummy to T.B. test the herd as soon as possible. The news we were selling our cows was a complete shock to him, as it came out of the blue. I also saw Tony Harris, who put the wheels in motion at Lodge and Thomas.

We had been milk recording the cows for more than thirty years, so sent off for the data for the herd. There was so much information about our cows, their dams and great dams. Generations of milk yields, butterfat and protein content. The sires of every animal on the farm. The choices we had made over the years about the breeding of our livestock.

Thankfully, all cattle passed the T.B. test. I can only imagine the complete misery of deciding to sell your herd and then failing the T.B. test, throwing all your plans awry and playing hell with your emotions. We had decided as we were only going through selling our herd once, then we were going to do it right. We had all the cattle clipped professionally, so they showed themselves off looking their best.

The catalogue also gave all the information for each animal. We managed to keep the news that we were selling the cows secret until the last day of September, when they were advertised in the West Briton, along with the standing maize crop that we were selling as well. We managed to stir up the neighbourhood once more.

The youngstock and dry cows travelled to Truro Market the day before the sale, where they were washed. We went to the market that evening to look at them, all clipped and washed, they looked immaculate. Our three children, Sarah, David and Frances and our nephew, Matthew, milked the cows for the last time at midnight on the eve of the sale. This was so when they were sold, they looked at their best, with full udders. I did not milk them in order to get a good night's sleep.

The sale started at Noon, 19 October 2010 at Truro Market. I stood in the ring, while David drove them around the ring. We had decided that David would drive the cows, Matthew would drive the in-calf heifers and our workman, Edward, would drive the bulling heifers. As we had decided to do the job right, they each wore a tie and were dressed smartly while in the ring. The first cow sold made 1200 guineas and set the tone for the sale.

The top price was 1820 guineas for a second calver that had calved a month. Most of the cattle sold really well, we were well supported locally and farther afield, I had decided that I was drawing a line in the sand and therefore we sold every animal, down to the young calves. We were not keeping any. It was over! Any animals that were not sold during the sale, either too close to calving or showing signs of ringworm, were sold shortly afterwards, either at the market or privately.

By 3.30 the sale was over, my thirty-five years of being a dairy farmer were over, I was physically, mentally and emotionally knackered.

Selling our cattle was not part of a grand master plan and we did not know how things would work out. Rearing other dairy farmer's heifers seemed like a good idea. I had learned the technique of Artificial Insemination during 1993 and it was a useful skill to possess. One of my friends wanted his heifers looked after and inseminated, so a month after all the stock had gone, we had animals on the farm once more.

Obviously, not my own, but dairy stock was still what I was interested in and heifer rearing gave me that interest, without money being tied up in my own livestock. I had another friend who was heifer rearing at the time and I had discussed with him the advantages and disadvantages of how we were proposing to make a living and what was a fair charge for the use of our land and buildings and for our stockman ship and skills. Some years later, I was shocked and saddened when this friend took his own life, as his problems, either real or perceived, became too much for him to bear.

We had not been idle in the month we were stock less. We had pressure cleaned the cubicles and installed rubber mats in all the cubicles. We had used rubber mats in our specific heifer cubicles for many years and knew with rubber mats, the heifers would not need any other bedding. We also swapped a tractor in for a 140 horsepower Massey Ferguson 5470. We considered that if there was tractor work available in the locality, we needed a tractor big enough to cope with most tasks. David was offered work a couple days a week on another farm and our workman, Edward, found another job, as we all got used to the new normal.

Ruth and I had five days in London at the end of the year, we tried to go every few years, just to appreciate the differences in lifestyles. We were always glad to go, but even gladder to come home. We would catch the train at Redruth Station and would spend the next five hours looking at the different agricultural landscapes, as we sped through the countryside, then gradually passing the graffiti painted bridges and industrial units, as we got closer to central London and then passing the high- rise flats, with the football banners strewn over their balcony rails, as we pulled into Paddington Station. This time we pushed the boat out and stayed in the Tower Hotel, overlooking Tower Bridge.

We packed a fair bit into those five days, having a tour of the Albert Hall, visiting the V and A museum, watching tennis at the O2 arena. Visiting the Imperial War Museum on the other side of the river and a completely different side of London than we had ever visited before, rougher and more unkempt. On one evening we visited the Winter Wonderland at Hyde Park, with the trees lit up with coloured lights, fairground rides, the many stalls selling food and the gay men walking openly hand in hand. A world away from West Cornwall at the time.

At the start of 2011, I was coming to terms with no longer being a dairy farmer, no longer part of the gang! I could not go to the local milk meetings run by Milk Link, or discuss knowledgeably the rise and falls of the milk market with other dairy farmers. Other dairy farmers were still thriving, while I had fallen by the wayside and failed in my ambitions. Failed my mother and father, failed my grandparents. They had given me the chance and I had blown it. I had always hoped that David would have been able to farm on a par with our neighbours and not followed half a scat behind, as we had done. I had failed him as well.

Gradually over the year, our bulk tank was sold and ended up in Bideford, our parlour was sold and ended up in Wellington, our blend bin was sold and ended up next door at Mudgeon. I came to terms with my negative feelings and came to realise that I had done my best with the hand I had been dealt and no one can do more than their best, however much they might wish otherwise.

One evening, Ruth and I drove to Perranuthnoe and walked to Marazion and back. We turned a headland to see St Michael's Mount, outlined by the setting sun and realised the beauty we had on our doorstep that we had never seen. We resolved that night to start walking the Cornish Coast Path, although it passes through Helford, some two miles from our door, we had never even walked the Lizard Peninsula stretch, something some of our self- catering visitors completed in a week.

Helford seemed a good place to start and from there, we walked towards St Anthony, along the south bank of the

Helford River, past Pagagarric and Grove beaches and as we reached the mouth of the Helford River, we turned right to St Anthony, where we sometimes swam as children. St Anthony Church, across the road from the beach and the graveyard behind. The graveyard where my grandparents were buried over thirty years ago, my father over fifty years ago and my mother last year. We looked in mother's special tin after she had gone. The tin that held the letters she had received after my father's death.

The letters written the day after his accident by friends and neighbours, many of whom I had known all my life, offering their condolences, expressing their shock and offers of help. The tin that contained my father's obituary, with the names of all those present at his funeral. The dozens of farming families represented, from all over the Lizard and beyond. Many of their descendants still making their living from the land, some fifty years later: The Lynes, The Skewes, The Luggs, The Trewellas, The Cares, The Pascoes, The Faulls, The Tripconeys, The Bloomfields, The Bowchers and many more.

The tin also contained the report of the inquest into my father's death. "Tractor Victim driving side-on." Grim reading, even fifty- three years later! The tiny card in the tin that unfolded to reveal two lines of poetry about an anonymous gentle man, the card my mother had kept for fifty years to remind her of, her Partner! her Husband! her Friend!

Across from St Anthony is the tiny gritty beach called Gillan, a lovely safe beach, where mother would take us for a swim during the long summer evenings. The diving board that was there on the rocks is long gone with just the concrete plinth remaining. From Gillan, the coast path stretches out to

Nare Point, where there is a coastguard station and Penare hills, where I spent a day sorting out electric fences some years ago, for one of my cousins who rents the fields.

Then on to Porthallow, a stony beach, facing St Anthony Head in the far distance and then farther on through the quarry and into Porthoustock, with the concrete stone and gravel bunker built on the left-hand side of the beach. Magnificent in its ugliness, and where ships could come in and be loaded with stone for various building projects. Another beach I would not choose to spend the day. Bleak! Yet a mile farther along is the beach at Godrevy, with fine black sand that draws the heat of the sun and makes it too hot to stand on.

Finally, the path snakes through Dean Quarry, now sadly closed and the quarry fenced off from the Coast Path. It used to be possible to wander around the quarry and see the huge tipper trucks and dilapidated old excavators rusting into extinction. Not legal, but possible. Everything is gone now, as nature tries to reclaim the land dug out over the years. The quarry, a mile from my birthplace and probably where my father bought his dynamite, in the distant past. Then out to Lowland Point and on to Coverack. A sheltered harbour, where my grandpa took me to a carolare years ago, an outside concert that was filmed for 'Songs of Praise,' and we sang his favourite hymn:

Will your Anchor hold in the storms of life?
When the clouds unfold their wings of strife.
When the strong tides lift and the cables strain.
Will your anchor drift or firm remain?

Our walking at this time was a bit haphazard, the next piece of path we started from Kennack and walked back to Coverack, thinking we were never going to find it, before passing the last headland and coming into Coverack as the Christmas lights came on. Kennack is the beach we would usually take our children to on Sunday afternoons. We would mark out our territory and they would have a fine time swimming and making sandcastles, usually with some cousins.

The last time I swam was at Kennack. One day last year, I tiptoed in, as the cold icy water crept up my legs, gradually up to my knees, then a little higher, then standing still, watching the wave come towards me with dread, until the wave caught me and my testicles screamed silently as they were engulfed in cold water and they tried to climb to higher ground, then I was swimming, "Come on in, Its lovely!"

The walk from Kennack to the Lizard, past the little cove of Cagwith and the Devil's Frying Pan and reaching the lifeboat station, with the names of all who had served, boys I had gone to school with and long-gone distant relations to my Gran. She had been brought up in the village of Ruan Minor nearby and as the dementia took hold as she got older, her eyes would light up as we walked through the door, "Albert and Jim!" or, "The Stevens boys from Cagwith!" Never, "Brindley and Chris!" Then walking onwards until we passed the bare fields, thin soils and broken hedges of the land around the Lizard lighthouse, where our walk ended.

During 2011, I picked up work locally on a daffodil farm, learning about a completely new crop to me and the idiosyncrasies that went with it. I worked on other farms, either with the tractor or manually. Heifer numbers were creeping up to around 150 as we tried to find the optimum number that our land and buildings would take. I did not want to milk anyone else's cows, I had been more than happy to milk my own, but milking other farmer's cows went against the grain.

Most of our walking on the Lizard Peninsula took place on Sunday afternoons and because everywhere was so close, we could take the car and the pick up and leave one at either end of the walk, or if it was a short stretch, we could walk there and back. The next part of the coast path was from The Lizard to Mullion. We passed fields that I had pulled grass silage from, while working for a local agricultural contractor, fields that faced Kynance Cove.

One of the most scenic beaches to be found anywhere in the world (in my opinion!) then farther on, three choughs landed in front of us, reminding me of crows with lipstick, heading off for a night out! Finally walking over the large stepping stones that kept us out of the boggy ground and reaching the cliffs above Mullion Cove.

Over many years, the unwary or foolhardy have been washed off Mullion harbour wall during storms, swept like flies into the maelstrom of water, not knowing their final hour has arrived, until the huge wave washes them away. Some get away with it, out on the wall during a storm with their children and they get drenched, but by some miracle, do not get washed into the water. Do they ever realise how close they were to death or just laugh at being soaked? Unfortunately, Mullion Cove is still claiming victims!

All along the Lizard Coast Path, I had either worked in the fields we were passing through, or, at the very least, known who farmed them and the next stretch of path was no different. Past Polurrian, Poldhu, Gunwalloe and on towards Loe Bar. The fields overlooking Loe Bar had been in daffodils and I spent many early spring days admiring the scenery, while loading up trays of daffodils from those fields, as the wind whipped in from the sea.

Loe bar consisting of a shingle barrier that separates the sea from the lake, which is known as Loe Pool. Both the beach and the pool are dangerous. The pool is supposed to have long weeds, that pull unwary swimmers under the water. I would not know because there is no chance of me entering the pool for any reason! There is a serious undertow along the beach making it dangerous for swimming, with many losing their lives over the years.

Again, I would not enter the water for any reason. Porthleven is a lovely place to visit on a summer day, plenty of places to eat, a scenic clock tower and the harbour wall stretching out from the sheltered inner harbour.

My other grandmother was brought up in Porthleven, at a time when the harbour was full of fishing boats and the area around the harbour was used by rope making factories. As a girl, my mother when staying with her grandmother, was sent to one of the rope makers to buy a rope for skipping. I believe it was possible to walk from one side of the harbour to the other by walking across all the fishing boats moored up.

My Grandmother died at the age of fifty- eight from a heart attack, probably due to her sky-eye cholesterol, that she passed on to her daughter, who passed it on to my sisters and me and now I have passed it on to both my daughters. Thankfully controlled these days by statins.

I have driven to the other side of Porthleven, Breageside, during a storm and watched the waves crashing into Porthleven from a safe distance. The milky water from the huge waves climbs the cliffs as if trying to drag the land into the deep. The huge waves are split by the sea wall, which is slightly curved and helps to dissipate the full strength of the sea, but they still race inwards, smash against the harbour wall and fly into the air, dwarfing the seventy- foot- high clock tower and then thundering earthwards, before the next wave moves in. More than forty years ago, two policemen in their car were washed into the harbour and drowned, during a violent storm at Porthleven.

From Porthleven, the coast path snakes its way to the engine houses at Rinsey, and it is here that I leave the area that I know. From here on, I do not know who farms the land we are crossing. I do not know their life histories or their struggles and successes, but I still farm all the land in my head as we pass by, wondering who owns the cattle in each field and whether I know of the farmers in one way or another.

Keith's Accident.

I had been friends with Keith Pearce for many years. He had been a dairy farmer, but had sold his cows and was working for my cousin, Roger. The day of the accident was one of those October days, there was supposed to have been a weather window and Philip had cut his third cut silage. The weather had then closed in, with heavy rain falling and it was a matter of making the best of a bad job.

The tractors and trailers were sliding all over the field and the forage harvester kept blocking up, as it tried to blow the sodden mush of grass into the trailers. After another blockage, we had cleared the drum and the chute of grass and the machine was started, with the panels open, to make sure everything was clear of grass. As the machine was winding down and despite being warned, Keith saw a slug of grass in the chute and whipped his arm in to remove it!

When he pulled his arm out, his hand was gone, completely severed above the wrist. As I watched his arm emerge, I knew I needed to remove myself from the horror of the situation, in order to deal with it. I backed off twenty yards and dialled 999. I needed to give lucid instructions and precise directions to the emergency responders as to what had happened and where the ambulance needed to go. I could not have done that if I was watching closely the other men treating Keith. A gibbering wreck would have been no good to anyone.

After what seemed like an eternity, the ambulance turned up and administered pain relief, shortly followed by a Sea King helicopter from Culdrose. Keith was flown to Derriford Hospital at Plymouth, where the surgeons decided not to reattach his hand, owing to the many strains of bacteria that would have been in the wet grass.

Keith accepted what had happened to him and even shaved himself with his left hand the next morning. It is difficult to know how I would have reacted if I was placed in the same situation. Just seeing what had happened affected me badly for more than a week, with my nerves torn to shreds. Keith eventually received a prosthetic hand, which gave him the opportunity to drive a car and resume working on the farm once more. Nearly ten years later, Keith is still working part time, doing the jobs he can and seeming not to stress over the jobs he cannot. He is still my friend.

I have had my own close calls, sometimes caused by stupidity, sometimes caused by bad weather or other factors that have made the job in hand particularly time consuming, which has caused stress and resulted in corners being cut, which has put myself in positions of risk that I would not normally consider acceptable.

Usually, I do a mental risk assessment before certain tasks, but stress and bad weather can make you forget such rudimentary practises. Getting older is another risk, I realise that I am slowing down and cannot jump out of the way of a boisterous heifer, or other such danger as fast as I once could.

The Tens B

During 2012, we continued along the coast path from Rinsey, past Praa Sands to Prussia Cove, a place barely altered over the decades. The row of fishermen's cottages, now holiday lets but largely unchanged. The small courtyard, with the walls of the buildings built in a circle, to allow a horse and carriage to turn around. So much history in those isolated hamlets. Then onwards past St Michael's Mount, Penzance, Newlyn and Mousehole to Lamorna.

Lamorna harbour was gradually being eroded away by storms and had a dilapidated feel when we walked through and probably has not got any better since. We reached Land's End. We had bought pasties for dinner and ate them in the lew of a rock, over- looking the Longships Lighthouse. One of those days when everything feels right with the world. In the lew of the right rock, with the right companion, eating the right meal, with the Isles of Scilly plainly visible on the horizon.

I have always loved the journey between Land's End and St Ives along the road. The small fields around Morvah and Zennor, barely averaging two acres and the road snaking through some of the farm steadings. I always wonder why it is just Penwith, that has the patchwork of small fields and why they are not found in any other part of Cornwall. Maybe they are so small for shelter reasons, as the wind whips off the sea, certainly there are very few trees that dare to make an appearance.

The old mine buildings along that patch of coastline also add to the ancient feel of the area, particularly the two engine houses at Botallack, built on the very edge of the cliff, with the mine workings snaking out under the sea. Geevor Mine shut as a working mine in 1990 and now a tourist attraction. We visited Geevor several year ago to see the Man Engine, a forty-foot- high mechanical puppet fixed on an industrial loader and in the form of a Cornish tin miner, complete with a miner's helmet and miner's light.

We watched him appear to come to life, stand upright and look around at the hundreds of spectators. I must confess that with Geevor mine and the sea in the background and my forebearers links to mining and the Penwith area, the Man Engine sent a shiver down my spine.

All along that stretch of coast were mine shafts that had been capped with a grid to stop the unwary from falling in. Ideal for dropping a small stone in, to see how deep the shaft was and if it had water in the bottom. Is it a boy thing?

Zennor to St Ives is a spectacular stretch of path about six miles long, it has spectacular views, but is not for the unsteady or faint-hearted, part way along there is a large granite bridge, spanning a small ravine, some twenty-feet long and four- feet wide, we could not imagine how it was placed there. We later found out the granite was placed in position by shire horses. A testimony to the skill of the men and horses that completed the task.

The path then follows the railway line from St Ives towards St Erth, a lovely walk, or a very scenic train ride. Then into industrial Hayle. Harveys of Hayle were synonymous with mining engineering and built the largest steam pumping engine ever made. Sadly, like the mining industry, Harveys are no more and the foundry has been transformed into office space.

After passing through Hayle, the coast path continues through the sand dunes of Hayle Towans and onto Godrevy beach, with the picturesque lighthouse built on a small Island at one end. Across the headland, we came to Mutton Cove and we could look down on the many enormous seals, sun bathing on the beach below. The next beach along is Fisherman's cove, a steep tortuous path leads down to the beach and it is another spot that I had visited while a boy.

It is apparently a nudist beach these days because it is so difficult to reach. I don't remember it being so back in the day and I think I would have remembered, even at that tender age. Fisherman's Cove was the last spot on the Cornish Coast that I had memories of from my past and from there eastward, every cove and cliff was a mystery.

We continued walking the coast path from Fisherman's Cove, usually on Sunday afternoons and usually walking both ways. Past Hell's Mouth towards Portreath there are two fields of approximately sixty- acres each, level and running out to the edge of the cliff. I suffered field envy once more! Portreath is a more industrial than fishing harbour and was used in the past to export copper to Wales for smelting and importing coal to fuel the mining operations. A bleaker outlook than the cosy fishing villages on the south coast.

Along that part of the coast, green copper residues can be seen seeping from the cliff face along with the old engine houses, are a reminder of years gone by. Through Porthtowan and St Agnes we eventually reached the long sandy beach of Perranporth. All along the tide line, were bright blue plate sized jellyfish. Thousands of them, whether dead or alive, it was difficult to tell, as they did not run off when they saw us coming. At the far end of the beach, we saw our first wrinkled nudist, well first nudist, wrinkled or otherwise!

From Perranporth, we walked to Holywell Bay. I had always thought that a beach was a great leveller. Anyone could travel to any beach and swim, make sand castles, eat ice creams, whatever took their fancy. Holywell Bay was the first beach I have ever been on where there seemed to be an air of superiority.

You could almost smell the affluence. I cannot say just what gave me that impression and I do not know if anyone else has ever felt the same way, but it felt that way to me. Our next walk took us to Newquay, which was as far as we travelled on the north coast as daily excursions from home.

For our next length of coast path, we stayed in Morwenstow for a couple of nights. Morwenstow was the parish of Paster Hawker, the vicar who built a small hut on the cliff edge, for contemplation, the vicar who held the first harvest festival, the vicar who wrote Trelawney, (the unofficial Cornish National Anthem), the vicar who carried fifty dead sailors up from the beach beneath and gave them a Christian burial after they had perished in ship wrecks, the vicar who smoked opium and sat on Bude breakwater combing his hair dressed as a mermaid, as a practical joke. He obviously lived a very full life!

We walked from Morwenstow as far as the Cornwall-Devon border in the pouring rain on the first day. The second day we headed off towards Bude, without food or water, as we thought we would be sure to come across a cafe in one of the many coves we passed through, as in our own area. We walked through the GCHQ base with the many satellites, that can be seen for miles from the A39.

Then we came to the valleys, steep steps leading 300 feet down to the beach and then steep steps leading up again. Every valley, a strength sapping, hunger building, mind wearing, thirst driving, trial. After reaching the top of each hill there would be a short level stretch and then another deep valley, absolutely soul destroying without food and water.

In her book, "The Salt Path", about the South West Coast Path, Raynor Winn writes about Duckpool, "If we can survive Duckpool, we can survive anything! Stupid, Stupid, Stupid!" Raynor and her husband were wild camping after losing their home and completed the path in two years.

Ruth and I were walking whenever we had a few days off and are still walking after ten years and gradually joining up the dots. Although on different journeys, I would say about Duckpool, "If we can survive Duckpool, we can survive anything! Stupid, Stupid, Stupid!"

At the bottom of Duckpool is a toilet block! We did not need a toilet block; we could pee behind a gorse bush! We needed a café that sold coffee and toasted teacakes. No Café! Ruth sat down and cried, as we looked up at the next steep climb out of the valley. I could have cried myself, but tried to chivey her up the best I could, "We will soon be in Sandy Mouth and then we will get a taxi back to civilization!"

Eventually, we reached Sandy Mouth, an oasis in the desert. After a good meal, we felt better and walked the rest of the way to Bude, which was the easy part of the journey, along gentle slopes and sandy beaches.

Although a hard lesson, that path from Morwenstow to Bude taught us a lot and since then, we have been better equipped for whatever was thrown at us. We carry a walking pole each, we have proper walking boots, we have rucksacks with lightweight waterproofs.

We have a coast path book that describes how far each designated walk is, how long it should take, a brief description of features along the way and a grading of four degrees of difficulty, Easy, Moderate, Strenuous and Severe! The book is a 2013 edition and is getting a bit dog eared but I would hate to be without it.

Morwenstow to Bude is classed as severe! I would go along with that!

We also always take food and drink with us. Plenty of chocolate, usually a meal deal (sandwiches, crisps and a drink), a bottle of Robinsons summer fruit and chocolate, plenty of chocolate!

The Tens C

By 2014, we were growing to love walking the path and decided to increase our ambitions, from walking the Cornish coast path, to walking the whole of the south west coast path. On Ruth's fiftieth birthday, we booked several nights at the Tors Hotel in Lynmouth. We had stayed there several times during the previous five years. It was our escape and a couple of nights there, when life was getting too much, recharged our batteries and destressed us.

The Hotel itself was a bit tired, but the location, set on the hill, overlooking Lynmouth harbour, was truly stunning and the view from the restaurant was awe inspiring. Dinner was fascinating to me as a nosey parker. As the wine flowed, the talk on the other tables became louder and more indiscreet! The seven deadly sins all made an appearance.

Three men come to mind.

The first was loudly declaring the non- existence of God! I was thinking, "We are sat in one of the most beautiful spots in the Country. We have the beauty of Exmoor behind us, with the streams tumbling through the rocks from the high Exmoor hills to the harbour at Lynmouth. The wood lined slopes to our left, lead out to the magnificent Valley of Rocks.

"To our right, are the cliffs on Countisbury hill, with their ever- changing shadows. The sun is kissing the horizon and sending a path of light from the horizon into Lynmouth harbour. You can see all that and have the wit to appreciate it and you think it is some happy coincidence!"

The second man was sat dining with a much younger woman, who was wearing a VERY provocative yellow dress, that showed off her wares to perfection. My mother would have said, "I expect she is his daughter!"

"Yeah! Right!"

The third man was dining with his second wife, who was trying to persuade him to manipulate his mother into leaving the second wife her expensive jewellery instead of to her grand- daughter!

Unbelievable! But fascinating none the less!

We started walking at Minehead by the coast path starting marker and started an adventure that would take up most of our holidays for the next seven years. From Minehead to Porlock and onto Lynmouth, through a valley completely obliterated of any form of foliage, apart from Rhododendrons. These had made a dense canopy that no light could get through and the roots were so tangled and interwoven, that it was doubtful if animals could have lived there.

At the time, there were attempt to open the area up by injecting the roots with round up, but it looked like an impossible task to me. I hope to go back there and see how successful they have been. Hopefully, when the rhododendrons are in full flower. I am still expecting them to be there.

We have walked from Lynmouth to the Valley of Rocks many times over the past forty years. Firstly, when we were courting (old fashioned word Brin!) The scenery is stunning, with the hills unusually running parallel to the sea instead of towards it. Castle Rock, a rocky pinnacle, perched on the edge of a sheer drop straight into the sea. Across the valley in a lew spot, protected from the sea winds is a small cemetery. A wonderful, peaceful spot that if by chance I finished up there, I would not be too disappointed.

We have not been to Exmoor for four years and I am feeling the call! Where we live is extremely beautiful and is undoubtedly Xanadu for many people, but when you live and work in a place, there are always underlying stresses, that do not allow complete relaxation and our needs are met by Exmoor and the Valley of Rocks.

We walked through Heddon Valley and up to Great Hangman's, the highest point on the entire 630 miles of the coast path. The walks that you remember are the scenic walks and the difficult walks. There were stunning landscapes all the way to Saunton sands. Saunton sands were difficult. Three and a half miles of beach walking that were knackering. Every time we looked back, we could see Saunton Hotel. A great white block that did not seem to get any smaller.

That Hotel seemed to be in sight for days. From there to Barnstaple and on to Instow, the path was on an old railway line, which made for easy walking. Westward Ho! I wondered if it ought to have been called Westward Ho? Of all the many towns, villages and coves, we passed through on the coast path, Westward Ho! seemed the only one with absolutely no character, no sense of identity. Nothing that I could put my finger on, yet soulless!

Clovelly was our next point of interest. We walked through on an old coach path called the hobby drive. Again, level, making for easy walking. Then Hartland Point and on to Hartland Quay. Probably the most desolate point on the whole path. It did not help that it was a grey mizzly day, but the huge hills towered over the Quay and the black rocks protruding into the sea, made the place feel very intimidating and bleak. While walking there to Morwenstow, we did not see the sea for the day, which did not help to lift our mood. BUT that was North Devon finished.

North Cornwall was a series of very steep valleys and hills, from Bude, through to Crackington Haven, Boscastle and Tintagel. Hard, tiring walks. Several things I remember about that stretch. The stunted oaks at Dizzard, perched on a cliff top, where they had been blasted by the prevailing years for many decades.

Tiny ancient oak trees, fighting the elements, in a never-ending struggle. In one spectacular viewing spot, there was a bench, commemorating a farmer, who had lived and farmed there and watched the world go by from that spot for all his life. A bench is a lovely commemoration to mark a life well lived!

Walking into Boscastle, we remembered the flood that devastated the village in 2004 and again wondered how, with many cars destroyed and washed out to sea and many people being rescued from roof tops by helicopter, there was no loss of life. A true miracle.

That practically finished the whole north coast. It was time to start on the south coast.

The Tens D

For most of the south coast of Cornwall, we could look back and see the windmills at Bonython and the large satellite dishes on Goonhilly, as a marker of the Lizard peninsula. The coastline was more mellow than the north coast. Less harsh, more child friendly beaches than surf beaches. More home from home. The first walk started from Helford Passage, practically two miles from home across the river and on to Falmouth, past Maenporth, Swanpool and Gyllynvase beaches.

Although they were across the river, they were beaches that we were familiar with. From Falmouth, we crossed the river to the Roseland peninsula and walked out around St Anthony Head, past the lighthouse that had played such an important part in my early life (also, the lighthouse in Fraggle Rock). The Roseland was a place we had never visited. The small coves such as Portscatho and Portloe were a delight to discover, realising they were, for many families, their special place, where they holidayed every year, their Xanadu. In Portscatho, we stopped in a small café for a break. The waitress told us there were no sandwiches as they had run out of bread. Thirty feet away across the road was a bakery!

Sometimes we would come across some incongruous sights. While walking near Nare Head, we came cross a nuclear bunker in a field, built in 1963. Apparently, you can explore it at some times of the year. It is some twelve feet underground and would have been home to three people for three weeks if the worst should happen, while they monitored fall out and radiation levels. I suppose the rest of us would have just been snuffed out. Thankfully, it was never used in anger and was decommissioned in the 1980s.

Caerhayes castle was another surprise, as it sprang into sight. It is a semi-castellated manor house, built in the early 1800s and set in magnificent gardens, built just back from the coast at Porthluney cove. We did visit it many years ago, when Cornwall Young Farmers Clubs celebrated an anniversary by having a garden party in the grounds.

Caerhayes castle was built to look good as a large home, even with the castellated turrets, it was never going to withstand a siege. Unlike the castles of Pendennis and St Mawes, built by King Henry VIII, further down the coast, that were built for the strategic purpose of guarding the river Fal from marauding foreigners and stopping them reaching Truro. They are proper castles.

From Caerhayes, the terrain got very hilly, through Mevagissey and Gorran Havem. We reached Charlestown, an ancient harbour now used as a film set. There was a film crew there that day, filming a BBC production called Taboo. We watched the proceedings for a time and then called it a day. We started watching Taboo sometime later, but it was a bit dark and grizzly for our tastes.

Par was our next port. Probably the most industrialised port on the whole path. Opened in 1840 and used for exporting stone and more importantly china clay, mined from the ground around St Austell. In the mid 1900s, 65,000 tonnes of china clay were being mined each year by 7,000 miners and exported through Par and Charlestown.

Brazil is now the place where most china clay is mined, with vast resources and cheaper labour costs, economically it made more sense to transfer the industry to South America. There are apparently plans to redevelop Par docks into a new eco- town. A far cry from the white, dust laden industrial port of the past, when the glorious green seawater for miles around, was allegedly caused by china clay particles.

We passed the Gribben tower, a vast red and white day marker as we walked into Fowey and although Fowey is intrinsically linked with Daphne Du Maurier and is supposedly a "must" visit, it did not appeal to us. If I remember, it was difficult to walk along the riverbank. Polperro was another "must" visit, but thronging with visitors, it was hard to appreciate.

I think the walk between Polperro and Looe was one of my favourites on the whole path. I had been working pulling daffodil bulbs for most of August 2017 and had an unexpected day off. We packed our bags and set off. A fairly short walk, with stunning scenery around Talland Bay, overlooked by Talland Church and then Looe Island appearing around a headland and then walking into Looe.

Another stretch that I would like to walk again sometime. We liked Looe, somehow, with its working fishing industry, it felt more real than either Polperro or Fowey. Further on we passed Tregantle Fort, magnificent in it ugliness and then the dozens of small wooden chalets along the banks of Whitsand Bay, built between the wars and used during and after the second world war, by families who had lost their homes in the bombing of Plymouth.

These days if the come up for sale, they sell for fortunes. We rounded the promontory of Rame Head and the coastline of south Devon opened up in front of us, calling us onwards to the next stage. We passed on through the beautiful twin villages of Kingsand and Cawsand, through the parkland at Mount Edgecumbe, overlooking Plymouth Sound until we reached the Cremyll Ferry in September 2017. Cornwall completed. We were tired yet euphoric with that particular challenge completed.

Norway

Several years ago, our local farmer discussion group went on a tour to study dairy farming in Norway. I realise that some of you will not be able to comprehend why we would want to and some of you may even find it a little bit sad. I can only say, that I have been on farm trips to Canada, Switzerland and now Norway and have never come back less than enthused about what I have seen and what I have learnt. It has given me the chance to see parts of the countries that are off the tourists maps and the chance to meet people from other countries that I have interests in common with.

There are approximately 8000 dairy farmers in Norway, roughly the same as for England and Wales. The main difference being, that whereas our average herd size is around 125 cows, theirs is 25 cows. This might make them sound backward, but this is not the case and in lots of ways they are light years ahead of us. For instance, in Norway, if coming from another country, it is illegal to get near farm animals for at least 48 hours. This is the quarantine period and is designed to stop foreigners from bringing in any nasty diseases.

We landed in Oslo on Sunday evening and soon discovered that Oslo was quite an expensive place to eat and drink, with a small cider costing £7. As Monday was our quarantine day, we were able to do some sight- seeing in Oslo. In the morning, we took a boat and went Island hopping around Oslo Fjord. The first Island we visited was Hovedoya. This Island was mostly a nature reserve with a ruined monastery on it.

It was a very quiet peaceful island with many benches around for people to sit on. A very beautiful tranquil place. The second Island we landed on was called Lindoya. This Island was totally different in character, it had around 300 small chalets dotted around it, either second homes or holiday homes. There were no cars on the Island, but it looked as though practically everyone had a boat. Again, it was a very quiet Island, but I think we probably visited before the Norwegian summer holidays began.

In the afternoon, we took a tram to The Vigeland Sculpture Park. This park contained the life work of Gustav Vigeland and consisted of 200 sculptures in bronze, granite and forged iron. Some of them very suggestive! Again, a beautiful place to visit. Finally, several of us walked to the Oslo Opera House, a very unusual building, made out of white marble and with slopes in every direction leading to the top, with everyone encouraged to walk on the building and enjoy its many forms and plains of marble and the spectacular view from the top of Oslo Fjord.

Tuesday morning was an early start, we caught the train from Oslo to Hamar at 7.30! Holiday? What glorious scenery. For a large part of the journey, the train snaked along the banks of the majestic Lake Mjosa, with the early morning mist hanging over the lake and with the trees and mountains in the background.

I have seen this railway journey featured in a television programme about scenic railway journeys. (Ahead of the game!) We checked in to our hotel in Hamar, overlooking Lake Mjosa and for the next two days we were looked after by Geno, the Norwegian Red cattle breeding company.

Tuesday was mostly spent in the classroom, firstly learning about the strengths of the Norwegian Reds cattle. For the last 40 years in Norway, they have been breeding cattle for health and resistance to diseases. Consequently, there is no BVD, IBR TB and numerous other diseases in Norway that are rife in the UK. I realise that minus 20 degrees temperatures in the winter may help to kill a lot of nasty bugs, but the Norwegian ethos is different to our own.

For instance, in the case of BVD, we vaccinate against it at the present time, but the Norwegians eradicated it ten years ago. If an animal needs treatment in Norway, a vet must come to the farm and treat it. This also applies to the dehorning of calves. This system and the fact that there is one milk buyer and one breed society and all of the milk and health data is stored on one data base, means there is a wealth of health data for practically every cow in Norway. This can be used when deciding which cows to breed bulls from.

Our second lesson was on Genomics. (I always knew that algebra must have a use). Whereas in the olden days, a stockman would pick out a good bull and a good cow and with a bit of luck would produce a bull calf that was worth breeding heifers from. Genomics is the new way of selecting bulls for breeding and they are chosen by their sire and dams DNA.

The bull-calves DNA is also studied to see if the positive traits that are required are present, and if so, the bull calf would join the breeding programme. Scientists and not stockmen are now choosing the bulls to breed from. The genomic method speeds up the genetic improvement in the breed and however unlikely it sounds; it seems to work in practise as well.

Following the lectures, it was good to sit by the lake for a couple of hours and to go for a swim. (Warmer than the Helford).

Wednesday, we visited two farms. The first farm we visited had 50 cows that were milked through a new robot. The farmer also used a robot to scrape the slurry. A very modern way to manage cows in a cowshed that was over 100 years old. The farmer also had a contract to clear snow from the roads during the winter, as a profitable side line.

The second farm, again milked 50 cows. Two neighbouring farmers had pooled their resources and erected a new cowshed between them, to enable them to milk 50 cows, again milked through a robot, as are 40 % of the cows in Norway. During the summer, this farm let their heifers up into the mountains to graze, along with heifers from another 20 farms. The farmer told us that this was not normally a problem, although one year they lost 10 heifers to bears. This is one problem we do not have in the UK.

Thursday, we visited our third farm, this one milking 27 cows, through a 12/12 parlour. Milking took about 40 minutes. In the UK, a parlour of that size would probably be milking at least 100 cows. In the afternoon, we travelled back to Oslo, had a quick look around the royal palace and on Friday flew back to the UK.

My impressions of the Norwegians, in general, were that most of them could speak English and they were very friendly and helpful, even in Oslo. The Norwegians we spoke to all seemed to hunt or shoot during the winter, either elk, beavers or red dears and 12% of the population are licenced to hunt.

My impressions of their farming were that they were getting 50p/litre for their milk and more in less favoured areas, as opposed to 20p/litre in the UK, with the Norwegian Government proactive in keeping farming profitable and working with the agricultural industry for every one's benefit. All the land that we saw was well farmed with a large proportion of the land in cereal crops and vegetables.

A very beautiful, well run, organised, friendly country that I feel privileged to have visited.

Walking South Devon.

From the Cremyll ferry, the path was urban in character, through the Royal William Yard, past the docks, over Plymouth Hoe and through the Barbican and on to Mount Batten, through bustling industrial estates beside busy roads. Interesting, but different to the main stream coast path. Then followed the South Hams, Bigbury on Sea, Burgh Island, Bolt Head and Tail, Hope Cove and Salcombe. This area was riddled with rivers cutting many miles inland, necessitating either ferry rides (if available) or taxi rides around them.

We passed Hallsands. The shingle banks off shore had been dredged in the early 1800s to build The Royal William Yard in Plymouth, leaving Hallsands defenceless from the sea, the houses had gradually and inexorably fallen into the sea, with just a few left partially standing as we passed by. Shortly afterwards, we walked into Torcross and Slapton sands.

During the second World War, 3,000 people were ordered to leave their homes and farms and move away from the area, in order for the Americans to commandeer the area as a training ground for the Normandy landings. In one exercise, German E boats attacked the American landing craft, sinking several and resulting in the loss of 700 men. This tragedy was not revealed for many years, for fear of loss of morale. Today, a Sherman tank, resurrected from the sea off Torcross, serves as a macabre war memorial in memory of the men lost during Exercise Tiger. Onwards to Dartmouth.

We left Dartmouth for the next stretch of coast in November 2019. Not the best time of year for walking. We came across a steep concrete slipway, that was used during the second world war to transport ammunition, from the store at the top of the slope to the guns at the bottom. As soon as I stepped on it, I knew it was a mistake.

My boot slipped and I went down hard onto the concrete, jarring my sixty-year-old bones. Luckily, I was able to carry on and I did not start suffering until a week later. We did not have many "incidents" while walking. I was saved once by a young German, as I stood on a slippery piece of wood to make passing easier and would have ended up in the next County, if he had not caught me.

Another time, I stepped back onto a bank that was not there. I was saved again by a good Samaritan, saving me from falling into a bramble laden ditch. We walked through Brixham and then the urban stretch Of Torquay, Paignton and Babbacombe. The town feeling quite dilapidated and run down, while the harbour was full of millions of pounds worth of boats. It always amazes me how poverty and extreme wealth can co-exist so closely together in such places. We finished the decade of walking at Tynemouth. Five hundred miles completed; we were slowly closing in to the end of the path.

Honours 2018

In early 2018, I had the honour of an invitation to a garden party at Buckingham Palace, in recognition of my local community work. The dress code was either a lounge suit, a morning suit or national costume. For me, it meant a new suit. If I was invited again, I think I would have opted for hiring a morning suit. I also wore a Cornish tie to make myself known to my brethren, one of which was wearing a Cornish tartan kilt. A bit far for me, but each to his own. Ruth also had a new outfit. A vision in dusty pink. Once again, we stayed in the Tower Hotel, overlooking Tower bridge.

On the morning of the big day, we visited The Shard. We had watched it being built on a previous visit to London. Standing at 309 metres high, it was the tallest building in the United Kingdom. We travelled up to the observation floor, 244 metres above ground. The observation floor was open to the elements, with fantastic views over London. We had the privilege of watching two window cleaners outside the observation floor. Ruth was able to have a conversation with them. When things get bad at home, I am now able to say,

"Things could be worse. I could be cleaning windows on the Shard!"

Money isn't everything!

We had been asked to travel to the Palace by public transport, if possible. We felt a bit over dressed on the Tube, but smug at the same time, Me, in my new suit and Ruth, with her pink jacket and fancy hat. We travelled to Victoria station and then walked towards the Palace, joining the many other worthies, who were heading for the same destination. The traffic had been cleared around the Palace and we were lined up in rows, ready to enter when asked to do so.

Fascinating, watching the thousands of people, all excited and thrilled to be there. Most dressed up to the nines for the occasion. I do remember one man who had a bright orange suit and a completely tattooed head standing in the queue. I did wonder just what he had accomplished to be there. Not being judgemental, just wondering what his story was!

The gates opened and we filed in across the gravel and into the Palace, through the doors that Presidents and Prime Ministers had walked through. John F Kennedy, Ronald Reagan and Winston Churchill. It felt as if we were stepping through history. We walked through two large rooms and then we were walking down the stairs into the forty acres of magnificent gardens.

I believe there were about 8,000 guests present, admiring the gardens, listening to the band and mingling. Many foreigners, in their national costumes. Several bishops, sweeping around in their purple robes. Many service men and firemen, smart in their uniforms. The tea tent was probably 150 metres long, with many tea stations. Everyone was fed and watered without any dramas.

The garden party started at 3 pm and ended around 6pm. Many had left by then, but we stayed till the very end, wanting to make the most of the opportunity we had been given. Then it was back on the Tube and back to our hotel, on what had been a very special day.

Also in 2018, I was elected as a vice president of Cornwall Young Farmers Clubs. Another great honour that I felt privileged to receive and the opportunity to help out where possible. In 2019, we were asked if we could host the Cornwall Y.F.C. county rally at Withan. I knew we had a good site, because several years previously, our daughter, Sarah and Alan held their wedding reception here.

A level entry from the road and parking in Upper Calanchard, a level six- acre field, with a gateway into Bramble Field, a seven-acre field, level at the top and then sloping downhill.

We agreed to host and after the second cut silage was taken, we were good to go. A large marquee was erected for the static classes, photography, cookery, handicrafts, etc. This was also used for the rally dance that followed proceedings. There was also a large swimming pool, made out of plastic lined straw bales, with a telegraph pole hung over it for a greasy pole competition.

We were fortunate to have help from St Keverne fire brigade in filling the pool, which helped things along. One of the competitions was to design the cover of my next book and I was asked to judge it, which naturally appealed to my vanity. There was also a competition to design and build a go-kart, butt, dandy or whatever they are called these days. The competitors then had to race them down the hill. There was a ramp half way down the hill, but this was deemed too dangerous and we dismantled it.

Several Young Farmers thought this was spoiling their fun and challenged me to a race. I was fifty- nine years old and I still did not have the wit to decline a challenge. They gave me a choice of go-karts. I picked one, got in it and we started downhill. What I did not know, was that a couple of them were going to push me as fast as ever they could. I was hounding down the hill a lot faster than I was comfortable with.

Thankfully, after many years of racing down our lane in four-wheel contraptions, I did not panic and managed to get to the bottom in one piece, without turning turtle. Whether those little beggars were disappointed or glad that I had not come to grief, I do not know. Hopefully, next time, if challenged, I will laugh and say, "No, thank you very much you carry on!"

When I was a Young Farmer, many years before, the county rallies were held in the grounds of stately homes, Trewithen, Pencarrow, Tregothnan and Killiow. Whereas, we could not compete with those settings, we were still honoured to host the rally and hope many present-day Young Farmers will remember the day and the site with affection.

My Sixtieth Birthday

I was probably in a better place mentally when reaching sixty than I was reaching fifty. I had come to terms with not reaching my earlier goals, of expanding my farming empire to the extent I wished and of selling our dairy herd. I was getting used to not milking cows and had plenty of other work. Ruth and I were both pretty healthy. The children were content and we had three healthy grandsons. A lot to be thankful for.

I was having three parties for my sixtieth. One for friends and two for family. All held at Withan. It gave me chance to see and chat to most of the people who were important to me. I enjoyed them all.

However, on the last day of my fifties, my bank took £18,300 out of our current account for absolutely no reason. I have spoken to many friends and acquaintances and none of them had ever heard of such a thing happening. I get a text message from my bank every morning, showing the latest transactions, so it was quite a shock. I rang them immediately, confident that the matter would be sorted without much bother.

Unfortunately, although they could take money out with no problem, they could not put it back due to the risk of money laundering. The matter had to go to higher authorities. That transaction took us well over our overdraft limit, in case you are wondering. It took them a week to get the money back in to our account, during which they had returned several direct debits and bounced my son's wages as well.

Obviously, we received some compensation, but the matter seemed to be dealt with very incompetently. If the boot was on the other foot and I had £18,300 deposited into my account, I am sure they would have wanted it back pretty damn quick. Money laundering or no money laundering. Why was it not possible to make a note on my account, stating that all transactions were to be honoured or at least referred to a manager, before bouncing them?

Thankfully, it did not ruin my sixtieth birthday, but it easily could have!

The Twenties

We started 2020 with Mother's funeral on 15 January. With 250 attending, it was the last proper local country funeral for eighteen months. The Covid 19 pandemic had started in China, when a bat transferred the Corona virus to a human, in a few weeks, its tentacles had travelled around the world, causing misery and death in its wake. Social distancing became the norm, staying two metres apart from everyone and frantic hand washing to try and ward off the virus.

By March 17, Flora Day, Royal Cornwall and Devon County shows had been postponed or cancelled, in response to the number of cases increasing rapidly and the death rate starting to rise. We were warned of a total lock down, starting on Monday, 30 March. This meant working from home wherever possible and firms not considered essential, shutting down. Schools were shutdown. People were only permitted to leave home for essential purposes, such as food shopping and an hour's exercise each day.

For many people, the last week end before lockdown meant a trip to a local beauty spot. Snowdonia was grid locked with traffic and in Cornwall, hundreds headed for Tregantle Fort, near Plymouth, with cars lining both sides of the road. I could not think of anything more stupid and If I had ventured there, I would have looked at the traffic and driven somewhere quieter or home. The virus loved crowds!

The government also brought in a furlough scheme. Those who could not work were paid eighty per cent of their wages in order to keep them employed. It is frightening to think that nearly 12,000,000 were claiming furlough, while doing no useful work.

As a farmer, I was extremely fortunate, as I had work to keep me occupied and to give me focus. In addition, we had beautiful riverside walks within walking distance. By the time Easter came on 12 April, the number of people infected in the UK had reached 84,000, with over 10,000 deaths. We walked through Helford on Easter Sunday. Whereas in normal years, it would have been teeming with visitors and boats, this year it was eerily quiet, with the sailing club pontoon and the river completely devoid of boats.

At the time, it was tempting to be consumed by news and this was not good for our mental health, so we restricted watching the news to once a day. The first lockdown was partially lifted on 10 May, with the schools remaining shut and many businesses remaining closed. We were not allowed self- catering visitors until 5 July, but did get a government grant to offset the money lost. By then the death toll had reached 40,000 in the UK.

By July, I was getting cabin fever on The Lizard peninsula. For the next seven weeks, on Sunday afternoons, we travelled to Penwith and walked the hills around Lands' End and St Ives, discovering places we did not know existed. It also meant we avoided crowds of people. We avoided popular tourist spots such as St Ives and Porthleven like the plague.

In September, we were ready to resume walking the coast path. Starting at Tynemouth, we walked through Dawlish, along the new sea wall, renewed after the gales in 2014 that washed away the old sea wall and left the railway lines hanging in mid- air. We then followed the railway line to Dawlish Warren. It was a glorious September Saturday and thousands of people had headed for Dawlish Warren for what would have probably been the last hooray of summer. Most of them had no comprehension of social distancing and we could not wait to get out of the place and away from the throngs.

Exmouth was next, another beautiful evening, with the setting sun casting coppery shadows on the skins of the young and lithe bathers, who were congregating together with their friends. They were the ones who missed out the most during the pandemic. I hope they can move on from the restrictions that were placed on their lives. They looked like they were doing their best to move on!

On to Budleigh Salterton. The soil had now turned to red and we had past the obelisk that marked the start of the Jurassic coast. We reached the top of a hill, between Budleigh and Sidmouth where the views opened up inland. Beautiful, fertile valleys stretching for miles, interspersed with corpses of trees. As a farmer, it did my heart good! We also passed massive caravan sites, not quite so pleasing to the eye.

Onwards through Branscombe and Beer to Seaton. A very steep stretch that was extremely tiring. We had decided to stop in Beer, but had met a couple in their mid-seventies who were carrying on to Seaton, so feeling a trifle inadequate, we made it to Seaton as well. From Seaton to Lyme Regis, most of the walk was through the undercliff.

An enormous section of cliff had slid towards the sea in 1839, mainly undisturbed since that time and being mainly woodland and dense scrub. We barely saw the sea for the day as we meandered along the path. There was a cold wind blowing in from the sea that day and thankfully, the trees sheltered us from it and made the lack of view a blessing instead of a curse.

By November, the country entered into a second partial lock down as cases of coronavirus were rising again. Christmas Day was spent at home, because of the rule of six, that made it illegal to meet in large groups. We were usually around twenty- five on Christmas Day. On the plus side, a vaccine had been developed against covid and was gradually being administered, firstly to the elderly and vulnerable and then expanding to the rest of the population.

There was a lot of negative publicity about the vaccine, with some convinced it was a plot by the Ungodly to chip and track the population, some convinced the vaccine would make you infertile, and some convinced it was to make general practitioners a lot of money. Some even convinced that the whole pandemic was a myth and in reality, the hospitals were all empty. I know that as soon as I was offered the job, I was off to the surgery like a scalded cat.

2021 started with another lockdown. It is strange how the abnormal can so quickly become the normal. I suppose we had work, space and were happy in our own surroundings and so the restrictions did not impact us as much as 'normal' people. Flora Day and Royal Cornwall were cancelled for the second year. I had not missed The Royal Cornwall Show since I was two years old. It was always a chance to catch up with friends and acquaintances that did not live locally.

A County wide Agricultural social event that had been going on for over 220 years and had only ever been cancelled during the World War years. Strangely, it feels as if the last two years have been compacted into one twelve-month period. Lockdowns, vaccines, cancellations, Rule of six, pubs and restaurants closed, masks on, social distancing, schools closed, opening up, lock down again, in a swirl of emotions, as the government tried to find the right balance between stopping the NHS from getting bogged down with covid cases and keeping the economy of the Country from collapsing. A fine line to tread.

On 30 April, I went to a large Asda store in Falmouth with Ruth. Anxiety! I felt like a rat in a trap. So many people, crossing in front of me, behind me and to all sides. Too close! Back off, I don't care if they have got masks on. Keep away from me. I know I have been jabbed, but I am still VULNERABLE! I was glad to get back outside.

June, up to Dorset to walk more of the path. Lyme Regis to West Bay, over Golden Cap, the highest point on the whole of the south coast path. Mist spoiled the view from the top, but at 625 feet above sea level, it was a long way up and a long way down. The next day, we walked to Abbotsbury, four miles along the shingle of Chesil Beach.

Level, but hard walking, with the crunching sound the shingle made really irritating Ruth. We had a picnic lunch on the shingle. It never used to be any trouble, but now when we sit on the ground, we wonder how we are going to get back upright. Leaving Abbotsbury on the way to Wyke Regis, we passed several lovely farms. The first was a dairy farm that we walked through, large parallel gently sloping fields that were sheltered from the prevailing winds by the large shingle bank.

Further on there were fields of phacelia, being grown as a green manure crop. Then several heavy crops of winter wheat. It appeared to be a very fertile stretch of land that bordered the fleet, inside the shingle bank. This walk was nearly eleven miles and although it was classed as easy, it was a hot day and I really struggled. Several months earlier, I had been diagnosed with heart problems. My doctor told me that I could carry on walking, but should not take up gig rowing, or renew my interest in Tug of War.

By the end of the day, I was questioning my physical ability to finish the rest of the coast path and wondering if we would have to walk half a stage at a time in order to finish it. We only had fifty miles to go to finish and I would have felt proper cheated if it ended there. The next day, we were walking around Portland, I was looking at bus stops on the map to see where we could be picked up if necessary. Thankfully, there was a stiff sea breeze that day, I felt infinitely better and it was a day that we both really enjoyed.

There was a sculpture park in an old quarry, with animals chiselled into the Portland stone, with many other quarries to explore and rock climbers hanging off a steep cliff, that I would not have gone near. We had dinner at Portland Bill, with the relief of knowing that I was not finished yet. Probably one of our favourite walks of the whole 630 miles. Then on to Lulworth Cove on a misty day. We climbed up some strenuous hills, as we neared Durdledoor, the mist was getting thicker. We met a couple of German walkers. I asked them in my best English,

"Could 'ee see Durdledoor 'er no?"

"I beg your pardon?"

"Could —'ee—see— Durdledoor—'er —no?"

"Oh! Yes, quite well really!"

"Proper job!"

Durdledoor was quite murky in the mist and there was a tall ship sailing by. Quite surreal and thoughts of smugglers and dirty deeds in the dim and distant past went through my mind. Thoughts were also of the young men who had jumped off the rocks at the top of Durdledoor at the start of the pandemic and necessitating the crowds on the beach to move to one end so two air ambulances could land on the beach and transport the badly injured boys to hospital. We then walked the last mile to Lulworth down a laid stone path that played hell with my knees. The circular cove of Lulworth was also swathed in mist as we arrived, leaving us unable to really appreciate its true magnificence.

Three months later, we were back for the final push. We walked on Lulworth beach, covered with white pebbles, to the far end of the cove, where there was a steep, slippery path to the top. We then entered the Lulworth army shooting range. 7,500 acres that were cleared of people in 1943, to enable it to be used for training soldiers. It was later compulsory purchased and is still used for training purposes, with dozens of old tanks and armoured cars dotted around.

The majority of the land has not been changed by modern agriculture in the last eighty years. The land is still used for training purposes and the coast path, as a rule, is only open during the weekends. We had left the red soil behind and were now walking by chalk cliffs, some of the path was frighteningly close to the edge of the cliff. One place, I thought, "Shit to that!" and walked a little further inland.

No one would want to come and scrape me off the beach. As we approached Kimmeridge, we passed a nodding donkey oil well. Surprising what you come across when you least expect it. From Kimmeridge, we passed the Clavell Tower, a building that had been taken down and rebuilt twenty- five yards further inland, to stop it toppling into the sea. For the life of me, I could not see how they had managed it. Striding Ledge was then soon in sight, with a swimming pool, blasted out of solid rock by local quarry men, for the local children to swim in.

Some places the path seemed to disappear straight over a cliff. It was heart in the mouth walking, certainly not to be attempted when intoxicated. St Aldhem's Head was in sight for several miles and it looked a level piece of ground to reach it. However, as we got closer, we noticed a dip in the countryside and as we walked closer, the dip became deeper and deeper. When we reached the dip, we could see that it dropped three hundred feet, nearly to the sea and then probably three hundred steps on the other side.

When we eventually reached the top of those steps, there were two first aiders with oxygen. Unfortunately, not for us, but for participants in a sponsored walk, who were walking thirty miles of the coast path that day. They deserved their oxygen, as that distance took us four days and I thought we were heroes. Soon we had reached Swanage, stopping at Durlston Castle to admire the forty-two tonne granite globe and eat the obligatory toasted teacake.

One more day walking to finish. Described as moderate, it was an ideal last walk. From Swanage, up the hill to Ballard Point and then a gentle stroll out to Old Harry Rocks. Chalk stacks, gleaming in the sunlight. We also had the spectacle of a red and white coast guard helicopter manoeuvring over the rocks, adding to the colourful scene. From there, we soon reached Studland beach for the last three miles, some of it through the naturist beach. We saw some specimens, but they were all ensconced among the rushes on the dunes overlooking the beach.

Be thankful for small mercies! We reached the coast path marker at South Haven Point with a sense of euphoria that we had actually finished, tempered with a sense of disappointment that our challenge was over. It felt like there should have been a crowd to welcome us in and perhaps a brass band, but there was only Ruth and me, as it was at the start and for all of the 630 miles. We took a selfie and caught the bus back to Swanage.

I believe the record for completing the path is about ten days, with fifty- two days quite possible for a seasoned walker. We had taken eleven years, during which we had walked when we had the time. We were not on a mission. When we started, Ruth was forty- six and I was fifty- two. At that time, we passed most other walkers as we strode along. By the time we finished, Ruth was fifty-seven and I was sixty-two.

Most walkers passed us as they strode along. My knees played hell walking down steep hills and I watched fit young men and women running down the chalk hills with awe. I winced with pain at the thought of it. We had met many other walkers in those eleven years. Some we had spent some time chatting to, some we had met just once, some we had met several days running as we passed and repassed each other, on our own individual journeys. Some, we had shared a taxi with. All had their own particular reasons and own particular time scales for walking.

The main difference in those eleven years was the great strides in technology. When we started, we needed a pocketful of pound coins, both for the car parks and the bus fare. By the time we finished, contactless credit cards paid the bus fare with a beep and a parking app on my phone paid for the car parking, with the opportunity to extend the hours if we were going to be late back. No longer did I have to shout out to Ruth across the packed bus,

"Got a pound 'av 'ee?"

For which she is profoundly grateful!

Walking the South West Coast Path, the longest walking trail in the country, is supposed to be cathartic and for me, I suppose it was. We had started soon after the cows had been sold, when I was trying to regain my bearings and find focus in my life. The Coast Path gave me focus and for both of us, a long- term challenge that we have embraced for eleven years.

I am glad that we are not starting it at this stage of our lives, but there are several stages that I would like to walk again, especially as since we have finished, I have had an invasive angiogram and had a stent fitted. This will not help my knees, but hopefully will help ease the breathlessness I have been suffering from recently. Steep hills will be a doddle!

History of the Land

When my brother Chris and I bought Boden in 1988 there was a clause in the deeds, set up in 1770 by Anthony Hosken (no obvious relation). It required whoever owned Boden to pay a sum of money into a trust fund to be used for buying shoes for needy children of the Parish. We had always heard that there was a Fogou, or underground dry- stone chamber on Boden land, it had been discovered in the early 1800s by Rev Polwhele, (the same man who held Captain Bligh of the Bounty captive in Manaccan Vicarage!)

During the summer of 1991, Chris was laying water pipe in the Fogou field and discovered a well type structure. It was lined at the top by shaped stones and was around eight-feet deep. Discovered in it were pieces of Iron Age pottery, made of Gabbroic clay, a clay only found around St Keverne. Also found was a possible Neolithic hammer stone and segments of a rotary quern milling stone. The Fogou was found nearby and was in line with an apple tree, planted on the field hedge, many years before.

Following these discoveries, the field was geo-physically surveyed and Iron Age occupation was thought to have been likely, in an enclosure of roughly an acre. Outside of the enclosure, a Bronze Age dwelling was discovered, with highly decorated Bronze Age pottery found inside. Most of the pottery was found with the pattern facing upwards and it was thought that the dwelling may have been collapsed ceremoniously and allowed to return to nature.

The Meneage Archaeological Group was then formed to study the site and evidence of Romano British occupation was found. Samian Ware pottery that was made in Gaul and the odd Roman coin, one with the Roman Emperor etched into it.

Recently, the Time Team television programme has made a documentary about the site and we wait for that with interest.

With evidence of Neolithic, Bronze, Iron and Romano British civilizations occupying the site, in a time line from 4,000 B.C. to 400 A.D. (rough estimate!) the questions are,

Why there?

What was the attraction?

Was it of religious significance?

Was it of strategic significance?

The site is roughly half a mile from Roscruge Beacon, which is an ancient barrow, either Neolithic or Bronze age. It has magnificent views over Falmouth Bay and would have been of immense value for defence purposes and watching enemies approaching from a long distance, giving time for the villagers to prepare or to disappear for a strategic amount of time.

The crug in Roscruge possibly means tomb and the beacon was probably an ancient burial site. Would it have made sense to have occupied the land around the Beacon? or would that land have been too exposed and too obviously seen from a distance. Would there have been a watchman on the Beacon at all times? Who were the enemy?

The site is also roughly half a mile from Gillan Creek, would the inhabitants have fished or travelled by boat to other waterside sites? Did they have various boltholes in the nearby countryside to avoid conflict? If some of the pottery came from Gaul and coins from Rome, there must have been trading by some means or other. Difficult, if not impossible, to answer all the questions from 7,000 odd years of civilization, in this tiny corner of Cornwall that I call home.

I have recently had the privilege of borrowing a copy of the Domesday Book covering Cornwall. Researched and written while William 1st was on the throne, between 1066 and 1087. At the time, the home farms were known as Desmesnes and the different classes of peasants, Villans and Bordars worked on the home farm in exchange for the use of their land and for protection.

They paid their Geld or Land Tax indirectly. The Freemen and Sokemen were higher up the ladder and had extensive rights over their land and paid their Geld directly. The slaves worked for protection, food and shelter and a former slave was known as a Colibert. They obviously knew their place in society.

The Domesday Book was so called, not because it passes judgement on doubtful points, but because once in the book, the facts were set in stone and it was not permissible to contradict its decisions, any more than it was possible to contradict the decisions of the Last Judgement on Domesday!

The amazing factors of the Domesday Book are how, nearly a thousand years ago, they had the ability to survey the whole of England and record the results in an ordered, concise manner that still make sense today. Without databases, excel, telephones, metalled roads, satellites or postage, they managed to accomplish a seemingly impossible task in a mere twenty years, getting the details of all the land ownership, the size of each farm, the number of ploughing teams and details of the peasants assigned to that land. Then travelling on horseback to a central point, where all the information would be collated and written out in longhand. Could we accomplish the same task today without modern appliances? I believe we would struggle.

What surprised me was the number of farms mentioned that were on the Lizard Peninsula. Some twenty- three in number, in an area that I would assume would have been one of the last to be surveyed, because of its remoteness from civilization. The Penwith Peninsula, in contrast, has only eight places mentioned. The twenty- three farms mentioned on the Lizard appear to be somewhat random, Tre- War- Nevas, Winnianton, Teveador and Gear could have been of strategic importance due to their proximity to the Helford River or the sea.

Others, such as Boden, Treworgie, Trelan and Trewince appear to have no noticeable strategic importance or redeeming features that would cause them to get an honourable mention. Were most present- day farms on the peninsula just scrubland at that time, or were they just lumped together to make for easier data transfer.

Were the Surveyors of the Lizard Peninsula transported to the area by boat instead of horses? Maybe that would explain the plethora of surveyed farms around the coast. Treveador was one such farm and at the time was held by wolfweard and was one virgate of land, amounting to some thirty acres (cornish acre is a different size to an English acre). Treveador had a track leading to Frenchman's Creek, so a possibility of loading and unloading produce if required. Treveador touches our own farm, Withan, of which there is no mention. Reading The Domesday Book has been very interesting, but it asks as many questions as it answers!

I was born in St Keverne and have never lived more than one mile from the river or the sea. Although a farmer, who's main focus has always been the land, I have always kept half an eye on the water and what happened on it. Until recently, I had never heard of the Barbary pirates. I thought pirates attacked other boats and plundered them; I was not aware that they captured people to be sold as slaves.

However, during the 1600s Barbary pirates raided many fishing ports around Cornwall, capturing the fishermen and leaving their boats adrift, capturing sixty men, women and children from Mounts Bay and selling them into slavery. Mainly operating from Looe around to St Ives, it must have been a very lucrative operation. It was not only fishermen who were targeted. During 1626, St Keverne was attacked many times, seemingly with impunity.

It does not take much imagination to think of the pirate boats landing at Porthallow or Porthoustock and rampaging through the countryside capturing the locals to be sold as slaves in Algeria, Libya and Tunisia, or used as Galley slaves to row the Galleons, or held for ransom. By 1640, there were reputed to be some 4,000 English people held in captivity in Algiers, many of them undoubtedly Cornish.

The Barbary pirates were at large for three hundred years and it was only in 1816 they were attacked by the British and Dutch. 4,000 slaves were liberated and the power of the Barbary pirates was finally broken.

Eight Hundred years after the Domesday book, in 1842, the tithe maps were produced. These provided the name of all the fields, who owned them, who was farming them, the field use and the acreage. Again, I have been privileged to see a copy of these maps and the information included, for St Martin Parish. Of all the farms included, there are only two that I can remember being farmed by a farmer with the same surname. William Richards farming Lean and Tobias Johns farming Carlauchard. I can remember both men, but both families have died out more than fifty years ago!

Other names of farmers in the Parish include John Banfield, James Lugg, John Davies, Henry Lyne, Thomas Roscruge, Thomas Hodge and Alfred Randle. Most of the names have disappeared from the Parish, although there are Lynes, Luggs and Hodges still farming in the wider area.

Our Farm, Withan, was farmed by Michael Sanders and along with the majority of farms in the Parish, owned by the Vyvyan's of Trelowarren. It is surprising that many of our fields have the same boundary hedges and the same name for the past two-hundred years, among them Slates (stad) Close. Bramble Field, Higher Carlauchard, Lambs Close, Parc Bullock (Bullocks Close) and Long Hill.

Of our sixteen fields, three have had a hedge removed in the past two-hundred years and these were all removed before my time. I would not be averse to removing a hedge, if I thought it would make life easier or safer, but our fields average six acres and having a twenty- acre field would be more hindrance than help. Two of the small hills on Withan were classed as vineyards, a complete surprise to me. One field was named Life and Death. The meaning of that is a complete mystery and once again, asks more questions than it answers.

The minor road running along our boundary was originally known as Carlauchard Lane. I have no doubt that lane was a rat run for smugglers in the past. Close to the river and a back road, with numerous quiet tracks to reach the many small landing Quays on the Helford. Several years ago, I had a visit from an Australian, unfortunately his name escapes me. He was researching one of his ancestors, who had lived on Carlauchard Lane and was transported to Australia, after being caught smuggling.

My Grandfather who farmed Mudgeon was replacing a floor in the house and discovered Bolts of Silk under the floor boards, undoubtedly placed there for safe keeping. There was also supposed to have been a tunnel from Mudgeon to the River, as youngsters, we cousins were going to try and find it, but life and commitments get in the way of such adventures.

Smuggling seems to have been at its peak between 1700 and 1850, during the time that the Tithe Maps were produced. Many of the Trelowarren farms in the Parish were sold in the 1950s, enabling both my grandfathers to buy a farm in St Martin. Recent and Ancient History in one Chapter. I spoil you!

Under Fire

Having reached the age of sixty-three, it seems to me that at the moment, Farming is under fire from all fronts. It seems that every time you turn the television on, there is a presenter advocating we all cut down or stop eating meat and dairy products, in order to save the planet. It is disturbing how far removed from the realities of food production so many people have become. A glib statement with no real knowledge of how the reality of a nation of vegans would impact the Planet. To play Devil's Advocate, we would need to remove all cattle and sheep and cull them, as they are deemed to be the biggest cause of global warming.

It would surely be unethical to keep some in a zoo and would be defeating the object of the exercise. Obviously, we would need to plough as much of the land as possible in order to plant vegetables, this would release millions of tonnes of carbon that is currently sequestered in the soil. The land that was not suitable for vegetable production, would presumably be planted in trees. As there would be no animal waste to use as fertiliser to grow the crops, more artificial fertiliser would be needed.

There would be a need for greater efficiency, larger fields, hedges removed, crops grown under plastic and thousands more tractors on the roads. The soil would also suffer, without the organic matter of cattle manure fertilising it and probably a considerable amount of soil would be washed away. With tens of thousands of acres under plastic, we could kiss good bye to our green and pleasant land.

Globally, vast feed lots in America and Brazil produce tens of thousands of beef animals, fed on wheat, barley and maize, many of them on growth promoters and hormones, to increase daily weight gain. Some feed lots are over 40,000 acres in size. We cannot compete globally agriculturally. We need to play to our strengths and not try to compete in the global market.

Great Briton has a temperate climate, that makes it ideal for growing grass and grass is an ideal feed for cattle and sheep. We need to make the best use of our natural resources. Globally, it takes 628 litres of water to make a litre of milk, however, in this country, rain falls from the sky, it is not taken from limited aquifers and water is not an issue.

We grow grass, we feed animals and produce milk, beef and lamb from those animals and then we use their waste to grow more grass. Sustainable agriculture that has stood the test of time for hundreds of years. The soil stays in good heart and with this system of agriculture, the myth of 'only sixty more harvests left', has no scientific basis, thankfully.

How many times do we hear farmers are grubbing up more hedges for efficiency and have destroyed the habitat for wildlife in this Country? In the Parish of St Martin, I cannot think of a single hedge that has been removed in the last twenty years. The map of the Parish today, compared to the Tithe map of 1842 is striking. Most fields have had hedges removed and now probably average ten acres as opposed to three.

The hedges that remain are the same hedges that were there two hundred years ago and still create wildlife corridors for small animals and birds. Cornwall still has around 30,000 miles of hedges. That is a tremendous amount of wildlife corridors. By my rough estimates, there are also 100,000 acres of moorland and 50,000 acres of trees, with the majority of the County, farmland. Three hundred acres of that farmland is being developed for houses in an area North of Truro in the near future.

One of my favourite views is from the A35 in Devon. From Honiton, the road reaches the top of a hill and to the left, the view opens up. Tens of thousands of acres of pastoral farmland, in a patchwork of gently sloping fields, interspersed with small wooded areas. I look at that view and think Nature could not have it much better than that!

In Central Valley, California, there is an area that was cleared for the planting of almond trees. That orchard is a million acres, consisting of 140,000,000 almond trees. Bees are brought in from all over America to pollinate them. There are strips planted between the rows consisting of mustard and clover, to help extend the bee's harvest. To put things in context, that orchard is bigger than Cornwall and has three species of plants in a million acres.

Rewilding is another current topic that divides opinions. I like to think that we have a range of different environments on our farm that would attract different species. If beavers were to migrate to Withan naturally, I would not have a problem. I do not think they would cause much harm, the stream on our border is surrounded by trees and marshy ground, so no farmland would be flooded. However, importing foreign species is a different matter, especially if they are apex predators, such as lynx or wolves. I don't think the walkers on the public footpaths would be terribly enamoured either.

Looking at the Rewilding Britain website, at the 12 steps to rewilding page, I realise that surprisingly, I am already rewilding, with a small r!

1. Do nothing; OK.
2. Gather information about your land; It has been in the family for seventy years.
3. Get advice; will leave that for the time.
4. Look at what is next to you; always.
5. Develop a plan; always planning.
6. Think natural processes; where I can,
7. Mimic natural processes; will hold on that for the time.
8. Encourage the return of native species; plenty of Red Kites around in the summer and cattle egrets.
9. Embrace the unexpected; I keep my eyes open for the unexpected.
10. Measuring and monitoring; I keep my eyes open to what is happening.
11. Collaborate and connect.
12. Engage and communicate; I write in the Parish magazine about what I am doing and what I am seeing.

At the moment, it appears that the Government of this Country have no clear idea about the future of Agriculture.

They appear to be dabbling with the idea of tree planting and dabbling with organic farming. They are doing trade deals with Countries that have different standards to our own. There appears to be no concern about our reliance on other countries to supply us with 40% of our food, especially at this time in History, when Russia is probably contemplating invading Ukraine and the fall out around the World if they do. If President Putin is prepared to send agents into Britain to kill people with an indiscriminate nerve agent, then he obviously holds us as a Country in contempt, which should be very worrying for everyone.

Surely, food security should be a top priority for any competent Government, with history showing numerous examples of mass starvation, caused by ineffectual and corrupt leadership in third world Countries. If we, as a Country, started getting near to importing half our food, I believe we would be open to financial exploitation by any Country that was supplying us. With 60,000,000 people needing feeding three times every day, the saying,

'Three meals from anarchy' would develop a new significance. When you hear that some families in Afghanistan are having to sell their children in order to buy food, it is a graphic illustration of what can happen when things go badly wrong economically and agriculturally.

It must be very comforting to many people to blame global warming on cattle belching. Cut down on your steaks and carry on as before, with no trace of inherent guilt. Undoubtedly, cattle produce methane, as they have done for millennia, but so does the 14,000,000 tonnes of rubbish that goes into landfill every year in our Country. Hopefully, as an Industry, Great Briton agriculture can not only become carbon neutral, but carbon negative, when there should be an opportunity to offset other industries carbon emissions.

We could become the cesspit to the likes of Virgin Galactic space tourism. Space travel is supposed to transform the participants perspective on Earth, which will bring countless benefits to life on our beautiful planet. I believe it would bring countless benefits to our planet, if they kept their feet on the ground!

Walk Around Withan

As we start walking up Long Meadow, there is lawn on both sides of the lane. These are flanked by granite mushrooms to stop errant car drivers and tractors from driving on the grass. Some granite mushrooms are immaculately cut, with their caps completely round, these can command a price of more than £500. I have seen a vintage staddle stone for sale at £1700. I believe that the majority are vintage. I know ours are! our granite mushrooms are more rustic; the caps stay put by luck and good judgement.

They are no showpieces. Although granite mushrooms are now used as garden ornaments, in the past they were known as staddle stones and did have a practical use. They were placed in a circle and with a lattice of branches criss crossing them, they made a base for a rick of corn sheaves to be built. The mushrooms kept the rick off the floor and stopped rats from getting into the rick and ruining it.

At the top of Long Meadow, we turn right into Higher Calanchard. Our top field is six acres and rises to the dizzy height of 250 feet above sea level. it is our only level field. All of the hedges around our fields are Cornish, consisting of earth banks that are faced with stone. We fence our hedges with barbed wire and allow three feet of growth on each side and the top of the hedge.

This makes a good stock proof barrier and is good for wildlife. Higher Calanchard borders the road and at the top corner there is a gateway that I constructed ten years ago, to allow entry into the field for the purpose of Sarah and Alan's wedding reception. This spot has always been known as Three Gates. Sometimes it had two gates and sometimes it had four gates, but it was always known as Three Gates. Thanks to my effort, it now has three gates again.

We then pass into Bramble Field, also known as Middle Pathway. This field is seven acres and gently slopes to the north. The hedges are pretty well parallel, which makes cutting silage in it a pleasure, as if you cut it properly, there are no short bouts. This field's hedge is the border between Withan and Mudgeon and as its name implies, it is the middle pathway of three fields, linking Withan to Mudgeon.

The lower pathway field is known as Stad Close. It is eight acres and an awkward shape for cutting, leading to lots of short bouts. The path at the bottom of the field joins our garden, however, thirty years ago when our children were young, I gently eased it ten yards to the left. With the children playing in the garden, we never knew who was walking through. This gentle easing made life better for all parties. The walkers had a much clearer path to walk, with less chance of walking the wrong way and I had less chance of hitting a walker with the tractor, as I was doing the yard work.

The footpath then goes through the Field Behind the House (pithy name). At the time of the Tithe maps, this field consisted of three smaller fields named Pound House Orchard, Outside Cave Meadow and Inside Cave Meadow. It was a very wet field forty years ago. It is still our wettest field and care has to be taken when driving on it during the winter. The gateway to this field used to be through the garden, with a length of string stopping our cows from straying onto the lawn. We eventually moved the gateway to a more suitable location.

The field behind the house was used for the dry cows coming up to calving during the autumn. Because of its location, if I needed to check a calving cow in the night, it was the nearest field to the back door. Usually, I would aim to go out at 2 a.m. If they had not calved by then, I reckoned thy would wait till morning. I was always a little apprehensive at that time of the night in case the mad axeman was behind a corner, waiting for me.

He never was, but at that time of the night, your mind plays tricks on you. Sometimes the cow would have calved, sometimes I needed to lend a hand and pull the slippery form into the world. Occasionally, more help would be needed and I would follow a cow around the field, holding on to the calf's feet and trying to slip the calving ropes over the calf's legs, with the calving aid between my knees. (multi- tasking) Usually ending with a live calf, but not always.

At Withan, there is very little light pollution. A slight glow to the north over Falmouth and another slight glow over Helston. Walking back indoors on any clear, cold night, I would stop and look in awe at the starry night sky. The Milky Way, with its myriad of stars strewn across the sky, its silky tendrils spreading outwards from its misty centre. The Great Plough in the northern sky, tilted on its side at that time of the night, where the stars seemed to pulse with the cold, in the inky blackness.

The constellation of Orion, with the Dog Star, Sirius, were also easy to pick out. My seemingly large problems seemed dwarfed by the scale of the constellations, the stars of Orion's belt were over 1200 light years away. The light from those twinkling stars had left the star before King Harold received an arrow in his eye. Me and my overdraft were like a speck of dust in the grand scheme of things. Occasionally, I would see a shooting star, as a speck of dust burnt up in the atmosphere. Then the short walk back indoors to the warm house and so to bed.

Back to our walk. The footpath then continues through a short length of woodland and then enters the Meadow or Roadway Field. This field is three acres and has a clay belt running through it. It is quite easy to lose a boot when walking through the clay and that entails hopping on one foot, while trying to pull your boot out of the claggy mud. This field borders the woods and it is my intention this spring to erect a fence, to make a path for walkers that will make it unnecessary for them to walk through the heifers. This will hopefully continue through the next field, the Long Hill as well.

From the Long Hill, we enter the Creek Field, a six- acre field that is shaped like an upside- down bowl, sloping in all directions. It used to be two enclosures when the Tithe maps were drawn. Emys Hill and Withan Hill. I have recently re-hedged a fifteen length of Cornish hedge that had fallen down. Time will tell if it will stay up! The Creek Field is the sixth and last field with a public footpath running through it.

A nearby gateway then takes us into the Eight Acre or Dry Field. The hedge dividing the eight Acre and Long Hill is reasonably straight apart from one kink. It is believed that the men building the hedges, centuries ago, would have dinner, then one of them would throw his hat to decide where they would finish hedging that day. Hence the kink. Whether it was considered to be bad luck to throw the hat twice, I do not know, but that kink has been there for hundreds of years.

The Eight Acre leads to the Lambs Close, a seven- acre field that has a nasty hilly corner against the woods. I nearly came to grief there many years ago. I was harvesting silage with a trailed forage harvester and trailer and had forgotten to engage four- wheel drive. I was pushed away with no warning and only good fortune resulted in there being no damage to both me or the machinery.

Back through the Parc Bullock and into Rod's Close or Four Acre. This field backs onto the farmyard and is particularly useful in the spring and autumn, as it enables us to run cattle both inside and outside, if the weather permits. We are now back to Long Meadow and turning left brings us into the Ten Acre. This field was three enclosures. The Gew, Well Field and Life and Death.

Although there is no well in Well Field, during a very dry time, when the fields bake up, there is always a strip of grass that remains green, running down across the field. Many years ago, I unhitched a trailer at the top of the Ten Acre and it slowly started moving. It rapidly gained speed, broke through a fence, travelled down across the hill and removing a small tree when it hit the woods at the bottom.

At the far end of the Ten Acre is Carnbarges or Lower Caulanchard. This field borders the road, the hills at the bottom were vineyards in 1842. Carnbarges was one field, but it made sense to separate the hills and use the level land for cropping or silage. Twenty- five years ago, we planted trees to make a permanent barrier between the level ground and the hill. (When I say level, I mean not dangerously hilly, not level!) The resulting hedge now forms a stock proof barrier. There is one corner that we cannot reach with a flail trimmer, the trees there are now sixty feet tall. If we did not keep on top of nature, Withan would revert to scrub in a very short period of time.

The next hill is the Ten Acre Hill. Very steep, with an obsolete badger set that creates anxiety, as I wonder if a tractor wheel is going to disappear down a hole and pitch the tractor onto its side. The final field is the Parc Bullock hill. Another bitch of a field that has threatened to give me heart failure in the past. Sliding from the top to the bottom, with all four wheels locked up, is not to be recommended.

After planting trees to form a hedge in the Carnbarges and Ten- acre hills, it was my intention, at the time, to plant a hedge along the top of the hill bordering the Parc Bullock and Lambs Close, however, a drastic cut of my milk price at the time resulted in the plan never coming to fruition.

The stream that forms a boundary between Withan and Tregithew is not only a farm boundary, but also forms a parish boundary between St Martin and Manaccan parishes. The stream meanders towards the river, finding its own natural course. For most of the way, it has marshy land on both sides, sometimes ten yards wide and sometimes a hundred yards wide.

The fallen trees that have fallen over the decades gradually rot away as nature takes its course. Further down the stream is a man- made, dead straight, leat that diverted the water from the stream and carried it down to where Tregithew mill would have been. There is no sign of any building left nowadays, but a mill stone was alleged to have been found there many years ago. The woods bordering the stream have many ancient cart tracks still vaguely visible, a tantalising glimpse into the past, as one wonders who and why they were used, both lawful and nefarious.

The stream then reaches Frenchman's Pill, past the small cottage where Daphne Du Maurier spent her honeymoon and under the small granite bridge that links the footpath from Withan to Helford. Frenchman's Creek is very narrow at the Pill, with fallen trees creating an impenetrable barrier to kayakers, it gradually widens on the way to its mouth.

The Creek was originally known as Treveador Creek. It is believed its name changed after Captain Bligh (of the Bounty) was found swimming in the Creek. He had been tasked by the Admiralty to survey the rivers in the district and was marking different spots with white paint. The locals thought the white paint marks were suspicious and could have been made by Frenchmen. They captured Captain Bligh, who was apparently too cussed to explain who he was working for, which ended up with him being held captive at Manaccan Vicarage and the Creek thereafter, being known as Frenchman's.

Legacy

During the last twelve months, I have been diagnosed with high blood pressure, diabetes, a faulty heart and I also developed shingles. At one point, I was taking twelve tablets a day. My doctor wanted me to start taking another couple of tablets but the stent negated that need. Since that diagnosis, I have changed my diet, lost a stone, had a stent fitted and hope, in the next few months, to cut my daily tablets down to just two or three. I would just like to say, that I have not spent the last sixty years abusing my body by any means possible and have always tried to maintain a healthy lifestyle along the way.

There is nothing like a heart problem to make you realise your own mortality, the fact that you are not going to be around for ever and at the age of sixty-three, you have probably had the best of it! You then start to question your impact on the world, both by your life and by your farming.

What will be my legacy?

In the future, will the conventional farmers of today, be castigated for their reliance on chemical fertilisers, pesticides, fungicides and other artificial substances. Or will they be applauded, for supplying nutritious food to an ever- growing population. I am always questioning my own farming practises and wondering what I could do better.

My grandfather Jenkin used to build a dung heap outside his cow's house. It was added to every day, the dung that fell off the sides, was placed back on top and the sides patted down with the eavil. After a couple of months, it would be steaming. The dung would then be loaded into the cart and tipped into dozens of piles in the field, where it would steam some more. Several weeks later, these piles would be scud around the fields, by then the piles were teeming with earthworms, that buried into and nurtured the soil.

In contrast, our manure is stored as slurry. Liquid manure. Liquid will not grow earthworms. It also has the added disadvantage of killing the earthworms that are in the soil, if you spread too heavy a coat. The advantages of slurry are, ease of management and as we do not grow barley, saving the added expense of buying straw.

We have cut the amount of artificial fertiliser we use over the past few years. We used to apply 4 cwt an acre of 27-5-5 (a cwt is a imperial measurement of a hundred weight and is equivalent to 50 kilos). This amounted to 108 units of nitrogen, 20 units of phosphate and 20 units of potash. Today, we use 1.6 cwt of urea. This amounts to 70 units of nitrogen, with the rest of the nitrogen, plus the phosphate and potash, supplied by the judicial appliance of slurry. Again, saving money. Another advantage of slurry, is that it soon dissolves into the soil, whereas dung would remain on top of the ground for a time, soiling the future silage crop.

Our land is now practically all permanent pasture, so we do not use many sprays. But, most years the docks cause us problems and some fields are sprayed to get rid of them. We do not wake up in the morning and think, because it's a lovely day, let's go spraying!

For all of our activities, there is a trade- off. We treat the cattle for worms, this enables the cattle to thrive and grow faster, without the worm burden in their stomachs. Unfortunately, the worm medicine also kills the insects breaking down the dung pats in the fields. There are certain plants, such as sainfoin and chicory, that have natural anthelmintic properties and reduce the need for chemical wormers. We have never grown them but they are options.

I do not think that becoming an organic farm is a realistic option for Withan. The steep hills make it dangerous to apply dung or slurry, that we would need to rely on. There are farmers nearby that are exploring regenerative farming, planting diverse species of plants, instead of just grass. That is an option that might be worth looking into, on our steeper ground. As yet, I am not qualified to judge and do not know the advantages and pitfalls. I know that at my stage in life, I do not want to be walking up and down our hills daily, moving an electric fence.

I believe at Withan, we have very diverse wildlife. We have woodland surrounding practically the whole farm and bordering the farm yard. During the late spring and summer, the dawn chorus is amazing, with a plethora of different songs. Unfortunately, little brown birds all look the same to me and I cannot tell the difference between a chiff chaff and a brownling. That fact is not something I am particularly proud of. I hear the different birdsong, but I do not know who is singing what! I know we have many owls nearby.

In the autumn, they can be heard hooting for most of the night. When we have cattle in the fields, the cattle egrets are usually around, along with the odd heron. When we are harvesting silage, there are usually a couple of buzzards flying around, along with seven or eight red kites. I believe that if the alpha predators are plentiful, there must be a pretty good mix of smaller animals and bugs, living on the grass, in the soil and in the woodland.

Last year, we sowed a wild flower mix in a patch of ground that was unsuitable for cropping. This certainly attracted the bumble bees and many different species of butterflies. Seeing them brings me joy and we have increased the area of wild flowers sown this spring. Little things that do not adversely affect my farming, but make a big difference to the diversity of the wildlife on our farm.

The question is, what constitutes a good farmer?

Is it the farmer that tops the market every week?

Is it the farmer that grows the best crops?

Is it the farmer with the tidiest farm?

Is it the farmer with the greatest wildlife diversity?

Is it the farmer with the newest machinery?

Is it the farmer that always seems to be in the right place?

I would not claim to be any of the above. I like to think I do my best with a difficult farm. I suppose what we are all searching for in the end, is the respect of our contemporaries for our individual farming journeys.

If I was to tell the thirty -year- old me, the position he would be in by the age of sixty-three, he would have been completely horrified and wondered why a man who was working all hours of the day and night for seven days a week, had not been able to progress in farming as he wished.

I do wonder how life would have turned out, if my father had not died at such an early age. Would I now have hundreds of dairy cows? Would I have already retired, in relative financial comfort? Would I be a better man because of it?

I am comfortable with my own farming practises and feel no need to flagellate myself over my use of chemical fertilisers and pesticides. My mantra has always been to produce as much food as possible, until the time that there are no starving people in this world. Hopefully, I have twenty odd years left on my earthly journey and I can continue farming, either until nature calls me to retire, or my heart decides to give up on me and call it a day.

I will then be taken on my last journey, Up Long Meadow!

1 April 2022

I had thought I had finished this book with the previous chapter. However, during the last month, Putin's invasion of Ukraine has turned the world into turmoil. It is difficult to comprehend, how one man's ego can cause such mayhem, misery and murder for so many millions of people. The barbaric megalomaniac revealed by his ruthless ambitions and complete disregard for human life. Putin's justification of the denazification of Ukraine, as a reason for invasion, would be laughable, if it was not so serious. The double ironies.

President Zelensky of Ukraine being Jewish.

The large Z' being placed on buildings in Russia and on dissident Russian's doors to mark them out. The symbolism to the swastika is chilling.

With many cities in Ukraine being bombed to oblivion and millions of Ukrainians, fleeing the Country to neighbouring Countries and beyond, the ripples of this war will last for years.

We are not immune, already in Great Britain the price of tractor diesel has risen from 70 pence per litre to £1. 10 per litre. This increase alone will add £5 per hour to the average tractor's running costs. The artificial fertiliser cost has quadrupled. The fertiliser we bought last year for £254 per tonne is now priced at £985 per tonne. We have three options.

We buy the same amount, perhaps spread the cost over six months, instead of our usual three.

We buy half the amount and give the grass a sniff of it, plus slurry to make the grass grow.

We do not buy any, harvest what grass we can and use the surplus silage from previous years, to feed the cattle next winter.

At the moment, every farmer will be playing out the same scenarios in their heads. With the majority of fertilisers produced in Russia and Ukraine, we may have the options taken out of our hands. The DEFRA minister, George Eustace, believes we can replace artificial fertiliser with farm yard manure and digestate, from anaerobic digesters. I believe he is living in Laa Laa land.

Most livestock farms already use their dung and slurry to the best of their ability to grow grass. There may be efficiencies that can be made, perhaps by using a trailing shoe or dribble bar and placing slurry directly on the ground, instead of a splash plate, that sprays the slurry into the air, before it lands on the ground. I cannot see how, in the east of the Country, where there are few animals, artificial fertilisers can be replaced, without a massive reduction in yields.

Great Britain agriculture, produces arounds 60% of our own food needs, which effectively means twenty million people in this Country are fed from abroad. In the worst -case scenario, of no artificial fertilisers, could that rise to thirty million, needing feeding from abroad. Ukraine is known as the bread bin of Europe. It produces enough food to feed 600 million people. It is conceivable that in the next couple of years, Ukraine may struggle to feed its own population, creating a shortfall in food production, that will impact the whole world.

In Great Britain, we may have the ability to pay for food from abroad, there will be many, many Countries that will not, the consequences of a 500 million people shortfall of food in the world, do not bear thinking about.

Successive governments have fallen into the trap of believing that it is cheaper to import food, rather than growing our own and the present government still seem to be pressing for more and more trees to be grown on good agricultural land. This has always seemed a short-sighted policy to me and even more so at the present time. Someone in power needs to grasp the reality of the situation.

Take a good look at the different scenarios that could happen and make plans to deal with them. Food inflation is likely to completely scupper the government's intention of keeping inflation below 7% and the price of petrol at the pumps will be the least of our worries.

As a young man, the worries of the cold war and the fear of nuclear weapons were always subliminally present. Those fears have been in abeyance for nearly forty years, only to resurface last month. I hope and pray that this war will stop and that my assessment of the situation, at the present time, is completely wrong.

As always, time will be the judge of that!

Acknowledgements

With thanks to my wife, Ruth, for her love and support over the last forty years.

My three children, Sarah, David and Frances, who we have tried to bring up with a work ethic and a sense of humour.

To my daughter-in-law, Beth Hosken, for the cover photograph, which was not set up, but just captured a moment in time.

To my niece, Claire Hosken, for formatting the photographs.

Finally, to the team at Austin Macauley, for their help with the book cover and guiding me through the processes in publishing this book.